THE SATAKAS OR WISE SAYINGS OF BHARTRIHARI

THE SATAKAS OR WISE SAYINGS OF BHARTRIHARI

TRANSLATED FROM THE SANSKRIT

WITH NOTES, AND AN INTRODUCTORY PREFACE ON INDIAN PHILOSOPHY

BY

J. M. KENNEDY

GYAN

Published by

Gyan Publishing House
5, Ansari Road
Daryaganj, New Delhi-110002
Phone: 011-47034999, 9811692060
E-mail: books@gyanbooks.com

Distribution Network
gyanbooks.com
India, USA, Canada, UK, Australia, France

ISBN : 978-81-212-9785-1 (PB
First Published, 1913

2nd Impression 2023

Printed at: Gyan Press, Delhi.

THE SATAKAS OR WISE SAYINGS OF BHARTRIHARI
Author: J. M. KENNEDY

THE SATAKAS

OR

WISE SAYINGS

OF

BHARTRIHARI

TRANSLATED FROM THE SANSKRIT

WITH NOTES, AND AN INTRODUCTORY PREFACE ON INDIAN PHILOSOPHY

BY

J. M. KENNEDY

AUTHOR OF "THE RELIGIONS AND PHILOSOPHIES OF THE EAST," ETC.

CONTENTS

THE SATAKAS OF BHARTRIHARI

INTRODUCTORY PREFACE ON INDIAN PHILOSOPHY

THIS new series of translations from Oriental works begins with the Satakas of Bhartrihari, and the object of this Introduction is not so much to set forth the very little we know about him and his place in Indian philosophic literature as to give the English reader some conception, however imperfect it must necessarily be, of what Indian philosophy actually is. It is true that Professor Max Müller—probably, in England at any rate, the best-known writer on Oriental philosophy and literature—has classified for us the six main systems of Indian philosophy; but his volume, which is one of the very few thoroughly trustworthy guides in English, is so ill-constructed and over-laden with detail that the average reader will obtain from it but a very cloudy notion of the type of thought to be included in the term "Indian Philosophy."

It seems to me, indeed, that properly cut and dried classifications are in this case very nearly useless to Europeans. When we speak of philosophy in Europe, however vaguely we may use the expression, we mean something which is not necessarily connected with any religion, and something indeed which may be entirely independent of religion, or even anti-religious. In India, however, the religion and the philosophy of the people are commingled to such a degree that it is very difficult and decidedly inadvisable to consider them separately. Furthermore, the Indian is much more logical than the European in that the theories he holds are his practical ideals of life. Very few Europeans, for example, have ever tried to put into practice the essential principles of the Christian religion which most of them profess to hold. The Indian, on the other hand, is not merely familiar with the chief tenets of his faith, but he endeavours according to his lights to carry them out in his daily life. Again, the organisation of the entire Indian social order is based on philosophical and religious principles, those principles which are expressed perhaps with the greatest clearness in the collection of writings known to us as the Laws of Manu. But in modern Europe our sociological and economic order has not necessarily anything to do with religion at all, and, in fact, in country after country we have witnessed the separation of Church and State; as if the two things, far from being bound up one with another, were reciprocally hostile. Political philosophers, such as Hobbes, Locke, Bentham, Rousseau and Bluntschli, when dealing with the theoretical or practical organisation of the State, either despise religion, or neglect it, or treat it merely as an incidental factor, of subsidiary importance to the State itself. We Europeans do not think it a matter for astonishment if we find economics based on one "philosophy," such as the Liberal philosophy of Bentham, or the collectivist philosophy of Henry George, or the Conservative philosophy of, say, Edmund

Burke; or again, if we are confronted with a different type of philosophy independent of religion, such as that of Schopenhauer or Kant. We are not surprised when we find political economists like Adam Smith and Ricardo dealing soullessly with problems of taxation, and no doubt we should question their sanity, or at any rate their wisdom, if we found them suggesting that there was any necessary connection between property, religion, taxation, and the social status of the different classes of society.

In India, however, it may be laid down as a general axiom that all these things are intermingled. Certain principles of Western philosophies and certain features of Western civilisation have no doubt penetrated into India, as the visitor would readily perceive from the slums and low women of large coast towns like Bombay and Calcutta, as well as the hideous factories which are springing up all too rapidly. But, as any friend of India, of culture, and of faith, will be glad to think, these phenomena of the Western world are still confined, with one or two exceptions, to the coast line, and the journey into the interior of the Continent will enable any interested visitor to perceive for himself that the characteristics which distinguished Indian philosophy, Indian religion, and the Indian social order thousands of years ago still exist with scarcely any noteworthy variation.

The distinctions between the Indian and the European are naturally very many, and it will be sufficient here to refer to a number of the more important. What is bound to strike the European visitor above all is the caste system, the vigour and efficacy of which have in no wise diminished. The caste system in India withstood the terrific spiritual onslaught of Buddhism, the combined spiritual and physical onslaught of the Moslems, and the English occupation. An interval of hundreds of years separated each of these strong attacks, and yet the caste system to-day is as powerful in theory and even in practice as we can imagine it to have been six thousand or seven thousand years ago. A system which has endured so long, a system which is so oid and yet always youthful, must surely be of unique interest. It is entirely contrary to the spirit of Western Europe. Christianity, which in politics is represented by the democratic principle, has decreed that we are all equal. Vague meanings have no doubt been attached to this word equality, and its signification differs according as we find it in the works of Rousseau or in a Papal Encyclical. The fact nevertheless remains that neither Christianity nor Democracy can recognise class distinctions; and, where class distinctions do exist, democrats never cease to preach against them. We have lived under this religion or philosophy—call it what you will—for close on two thousand years, and if the time has not yet arrived it is certainly approaching very rapidly when all class distinctions, in theory at any rate, will cease to be recognised. It is still remarkable, as I am ready to admit, to find how many classes have remained unaffected by this theory of equality which has been propagated for so long. In Russia and Poland, and—though to a much less extent—in Germany, Italy, France, and Spain, there are still very perceptible distinctions between the various classes of society. These distinctions, however, are not recognised by the religious philosophy preached in Europe, and assuming even the maintenance, if not necessarily the increase of the authority of this religious philosophy, such distinctions are in time bound to disappear.

Now, in India there are not merely distinctions between the various classes in the social order, but these distinctions are definitely fixed in the religion, the philosophy, and the law codes of the people. Equal rights and privileges for all do not merely not exist : they are unheard of, and would with difficulty be understood by the people. We shall better understand how this system works when we come to know the four great castes into which Indian society has been divided for untold ages. First of all comes the priestly caste, the Brahmins. Although we refer to the Brahmins as the priestly caste, we must here make the word "priestly" include not merely priests as the word is used in Europe, but philosophers, learned men, and ascetics. Second in order comes the Kshattriya caste, the Kshattriyas of old including those now better known perhaps as the Rajputs, i.e. the kings, administrators, statesmen, warriors, and fighting men generally. It must be recollected that the kings and statesmen, however powerful they might be, could not and cannot exercise complete and entire authority in India. They have always been subject to the spiritual authority of the caste above them. Thirdly come the Vaishyas, this caste including all merchants, business men, bankers, shopkeepers, farmers, and so forth. Lastly we have the Sudra caste, and this is a caste which it is difficult to define exactly. We cannot call them the working classes, because there are no people in India corresponding exactly to those indicated by the Western use of the term. To describe the Sudras as casual labourers would be to convey but an approximate idea of a small section of the caste. It is perhaps best to say that the Sudras are composed of the lowest classes in Indian society, but they are nevertheless a caste by themselves, and as such have certain privileges, however few and unimportant, of which they cannot be deprived.

Each caste is naturally still further subdivided, and there are distinctions more or less minute, with which it is hardly necessary to trouble the European reader. But it should be added that the variety of Indian society, like the variety of Indian scenery, climate and soil, is inexhaustible. There is a passage in Mr Meredith Townsend's book "Asia and Europe" which well sums up this variety :—

Indian society is not a democracy. Amidst all the peasants and officials stand hundreds, or rather thousands, of families as distinct from the masses as the Percys from English labourers, three hundred of them ruling States large or small—one is bigger than the British Isles; one only two miles square—three thousand of them perhaps who on the Continent would be accounted nobles, some with pedigrees like those of the Massimi or the Zichy's, some only of yesterday; but all as utterly separated from the people as a hill from the river at its base. And behind them stand other thousands of squires, each with his own family traditions, each with hereditary tenantry, each with some position and character and speciality which, within fifty miles of his home, are as well known as those of the Egertons in Cheshire, or the Luttrells in West Somerset. And behind them again are millions—literally millions—of families, country and urban, with modest means, and little wish for advancement, yet freeholders to a man, with histories often which trace back further than those of the Lords, with a pride of their own which is immovable, and with characters that for five miles are known and reckoned on, and, so to speak, *expected* as regularly and as accurately as if they were Hohenzollerns in Brandenburg. Ask the settlement officers—who alone among Indian officials, except sometimes the highest, really know the people—and they will tell you that, above the very lowest, no two Indian families are alike in rank or character or reputation, or even, though that seems so impossible, in means.

These features represent a trait of character which has been called, more particularly since Nietzsche's time, aristocratic. When we use the words democratic and aristocratic in this respect, however, we must take care to distinguish between their philosophical and their political signification. When we speak of an aristocratic society in this connection, we now generally mean by the expression what Nietzsche himself meant by it—a society that believes in a long scale of gradations of rank and differences of worth amongst human beings and a society likewise which is based on some form of slavery. A democratic society is of course the opposite of this, a society that does not believe in gradations of rank and seeks to level all classes. The types of mind produced in each form of society naturally vary: the aristocratic thinker, as Nietzsche expresses it, will be constantly looking down on the lower class as his subordinates and instruments, whom he will command in accordance with his wishes and keep at a respectful distance from him, and this in its turn will give rise to the longing for a continually new widening of distance within the soul itself and "the formation of ever higher, rarer, further, more extended, more comprehensive states," i.e. the "self-surmounting of man." The aristocratic sage, thus thrown as it were on his own philosophical resources, is bound to develop his individuality, his own peculiar form of expression, or, to sum it up in one word, his individuum, to a much greater extent than the democratic thinker can do. For refined egotism is not permitted to the latter, who must necessarily be altruistic and keep his fellow-creatures in mind as well as his own development.

When this philosophical distinction between two words which are now more often employed in a political than in a philosophical signification is thoroughly grasped, it will be seen what an enormous influence on the development of thought was exercised by the primitive Indian organisation of society. It is easy for us at the present day, with the works of a long line of philosophers from the early Indians to Aristotle, and from Aristotle down to Kant and Bergson, at our command, to talk glibly about the differences between aristocratic and democratic philosophy and the numerous subdivisions in each. We have within reach the works of both types of men, and there is always the possibility of our being convinced by one or the other, and having our opinions and ideas influenced accordingly. But it was a different matter in the case of the men whose works it is hoped to publish from time to time in this series. We may not know the names of the writers of the Vedas and the Upanishads, but we do nevertheless possess these works, which stand at the head of the long line of Indian philosophical writings. These works, with innumerable others, were handed down in what Max Müller has happily called mnemonic literature; for in ancient India the memory was developed to an extent which we in our day and country would consider almost incredible. It is safe to say that the Vedas can be traced back for at least seven thousand years, and I think that most scholars and students of Orientalia now agree in believing this to be a conservative estimate. But long before a line of the Vedas was committed to memory the clans which were as yet forming their philosophy only subconsciously were fighting their way into Northern India over the Pamir plateau. The exact date of this vast incursion will now probably never be known, and even its approximate era is still a matter of more or less haphazard speculation. On the basis of the most recent geological, ethnological, and philological data, most of us who are interested in these matters assume the Aryan invasion to have taken place not less than five hundred centuries ago. Yet even then there was a certain hierarchy among the invaders. They were divided—I will not say into two castes, because caste is often a misleading word—but rather into two sociological groups: the warriors and powerful men of the different tribes, and the herdsmen and agriculturalists who followed their leadership.

I have said that during this period of invasion a philosophy was being subconsciously formed; but it did not actually mature until the aborigines in Northern India had been subdued and turned into slaves, and until the Aryans had definitely seized on certain lands and settled there, and given up their wandering habits. This would naturally lead to the almost simultaneous development of the two supplementary castes or classes. The definite possession of land would naturally tend to distinguish the farmers or Vaishya caste from the fighting or Kshattriya caste. The lowest caste, or Sudras, were naturally looked upon as being on an infinitely lower level than the two higher classes, because primarily and above all there was a difference of blood between them and their conquerors, exactly as there was a difference of blood, though not nearly to the same extent, between the Kshattriyas and the Vaishyas. Simultaneously with the formation of the Sudra caste, however, and the sharper distinction between the Kshattriyas and the Vaishyas, the need for a higher caste was felt, owing to the necessity for better guidance. This necessity followed as a matter of course. We know how relatively easy it is to support life in most parts of agricultural India at the present day, and with a much smaller population and a fresher soil life thousands of years ago in the great sub-continent must have been practically self-supporting. The warriors, once the aborigines had been definitely conquered, found little necessity for continuous fighting until in later ages they began to fight among themselves. Two important factors, therefore, contributed to the development of the spiritual Brahmin caste. The first and less important was the fact that although physical fighting was less necessary intellectual combats in the form of administration were about to be fought, for the lower classes of the State had to be kept in order by the higher, and something more than mere brute force is always essential for this. The second factor, which was by far the more important, was that natural impulse in the soul of man that makes him look instinctively to some higher power; the impulse that leads to animism, totemism, fetichism, or any of the other numerous primitive forms of spiritual expression. It thus came about that we find in one of the early Upanishads the question set forth almost in the same words as it appears in the writings of the Greek philosophers or the Chinese philosophers and the philosophers of modern Europe; questions which must have been asked for thousands of years before they were at length written down in a permanent form: Whence are we born? How do we live? Whither are we going?

Now, all the evidence we have goes to show that the first men of profound spiritual insight who set themselves to solve these problems as best they might sprang from the most aristocratic of the warrior clans. In the course of time they and their wives and families formed an entirely separate caste. They naturally intermarried and thus cut themselves off even by blood from what had formerly been the highest caste in the social order. Their aristocratic upbringing naturally accompanied them and influenced them, whence it followed that the earliest Indian philosophy, thousands of years before a single one of its tenets was committed to paper, and even generations before any part of it was committed to memory, assumed a distinctly aristocratic trend. These early thinkers had no means at their disposal such as we have: they were not surrounded by the works of learned men, and the first generation of them could not be said even to have possessed the society of learned men. Instinctively faithful to the true Indian ideal, they quietly renounced what they looked upon as the delusive pleasures of this world, gave themselves up to a solitary existence in forests or in mountain-caves, and spent their time in meditation. And from such beginnings sprang the most wonderful philosophical fabric ever reared.

One feature of the rise of the Brahmins may be mentioned here, although it did not take place until long after the period which has just been referred to. When the numbers of the Brahmins had considerably increased and they alone had the privilege of interpreting religious beliefs, philosophical tenets, and the law codes to the other castes, they wished to arrogate to themselves the supreme power in the State, not merely in fact, but also in name. This pretension was almost at once disputed by the warrior caste, and Indian society would appear to have been shaken to its very depths by fierce battles fought with physical rather than intellectual weapons between the warriors who wished to be priests and the priests who showed that on occasion they could act as warriors. More remarkable still perhaps is the fact that the warrior caste seems to have been utterly defeated and in fact all but annihilated by the Brahmins. Just before it was too late, however, the priests perceived the error of which they had very nearly been guilty. Intellectual life is impossible if the thinker is brought into daily touch with the coarser side of existence, with the details of administration, with the mob and the ways of the mob. An intelligent executive is nevertheless necessary, and it must be interposed between those who think and the vast crowd of the common people. This intelligent executive had been supplied in India by the statesmen and warrior caste. If this caste had been completely ruined, its place would have had to be taken by the Brahmins themselves, and it is obvious that administrative functions would have left neither time nor opportunity for the progress of culture or the development of thought. Before it was too late, therefore, the Brahmins gathered together the fragments, as it were, of the warrior caste, definitely imposed certain functions upon it, and then went back to their forests and their caves. This is a unique event, and is worthy of more than a mere passing glance. It is no doubt true that culture and philosophy have existed in Europe, to take an example with which we should be fairly familiar, for more than twenty centuries. But even those among us who do not profess to be very ardent students of the classics will be the first to admit that we have not developed in a cultural or philosophical sense beyond where the ancient Greeks left off: we have, it is true, made great strides in purely material things, but in spiritual affairs we are little wiser than Plato, Herakleitus, or Pythagoras. And in England, above all, spiritual knowledge has been on a low level since the days of Elizabeth, not because high-minded men were lacking among us, but because their energies were overpowered by men who from the standpoint of the soul were on a lower level than themselves, and driven into paths for which they were not precisely fitted—first of all, the capture and colonising of distant lands, and consequently the administration of the lands thus acquired. There is in every country a certain proportion of intellect. In India, Greece, and France, to name three instances, a proper proportion of this intellect was directed in suitable and adequate cultural channels; but the limited supply of this intellectual force in England has long been diverted to administrative functions, with the result that practically none of it is left to carry on our cultural traditions.

This mistake, as we have seen, the Brahmins avoided just in time. They thought, which is a difficult task; and they left it to the intelligent classes immediately below them to act, which is a less difficult task. Hence there is from the very beginning of Indian thought down practically to the present day a steady spiritual progress. There is one definite traditional line; for without tradition there can be neither art nor philosophy nor literature. Occasionally there were Indian philosophers who shot off at a tangent, just as there were others whose footsteps often stumbled and hesitated as they advanced, but in general this line was followed by all Indian thinkers. It is a somewhat difficult matter to explain to the European precisely what this traditional line of Indian thought is; yet it must be explained as adequately as possible before the various aspects of Indian philosophy can be properly grasped. Let the following serve as an attempt to condense the essential principle of Hindu religious philosophy into a fairly intelligible form :

Matter follows the spirit, and consequently the spirit, or as we Europeans would perhaps say the soul, being the spiritual part of the body, is more important, infinitely more important, than the mere physical body. This unimportant physical body of ours may date, if we like to say so, from the moment if its birth, but the only important part of us, that is, the soul, does not date from the birth of the mere body, but from all eternity. Our body is born and dies, but we are reincarnated time after time by the only sensory part of us, viz. the soul, which is transmigrated or reincarnated from body to body.

Our soul cannot be looked upon as a

created thing, for if it were created, it would be liable to perish and decay, whereas it is really permanent. Not being a creation, therefore, our soul must be properly described as an emanation. From what then does our soul emanate? From Infinity—not precisely from that which in the Christian Scriptures is called Chaos. This infinity, or rather this state of infinity, is known to Hindu philosophers by the neuter word Brahman—a very different thing, it must be recollected, from the God we afterwards come to know as Brahma. This infinity, or Brahman, is the origin—in so far as the subtle metaphysics of Indian philosophy will allow us to speak of an origin at all—of all things. Brahman is even the origin of God—the most remarkable philosophic principle ever conceived, and one that takes a stride further back into the primitive development of mankind than any other religion.

Whether or not God is endowed with the function of creating does not matter when we wish to consider the soul, because the soul, like God himself, is an emanation from Brahman. The soul is thus self-existent, but being beyond the influence of matter, and being likewise an emanation, it is continually struggling to rid itself from matter altogether—i.e. from the body—and to get back to its source in order to become again one with the Infinite. Only when it has been thus absorbed by the Infinite again does it attain to its full state of bliss.

It may be held by Europeans that this is in direct contradiction to the aristocratic development of the Indian individuum, and that the soul, by thus once again becoming one with the Infinite, entirely loses its own individuality. But there are innumerable answers to this objection, and they may be concisely summed up when we say that, although the soul may experience a certain amount of happiness in sharing the consciousness of body after body, it must necessarily experience infinitely more happiness, incalculable happiness in fact, when it is in a position to share the consciousness of the entire universe.

This happiness may eventually be attained by the soul, but owing to the evil actions of men on earth it naturally follows that they —i.e. the spiritual part of them, their souls

—cannot attain to this universal happiness all at once. In some cases hundreds of thousands of generations must elapse and in other cases hundreds of thousands of years. Hence the calmness with which the Hindu will endure suffering and pain and cruelty, and hence also the calmness with which he will contemplate the pain and suffering of his fellows, and the infliction of cruelty upon them; for sympathy, as we understand the word and the thing in the West, is all but unknown in the East. If a Hindu is stricken with disease or is treated with the grossest injustice, or is plunged into the depths of misery and despair by the loss of parents, wife, children, or property, he does not utter mournful complaints about the injustice of fate. He realises that one of two things is happening to him, or possibly even both at once: he is being punished, and justly punished, no doubt, for his evil actions in a former existence, although his memory does not extend so far back as this previous incarnation, and he has forgotten his wickedness; or else he is being punished in order that he may acquire merit, and so live a better life when his soul leaves its present abode and passes into some other earthly habitation.

This emanation of the soul from the Infinite, and its continual reincarnation in body after body until it has acquired sufficient merit to return to the Infinite again, is the traditional principle of Hindu religion and philosophy, and I have tried to explain it as clearly as possible. One question, however, will instantly suggest itself to the reader, viz. what process must the soul go through in order that it may acquire sufficient merit, to use the well-known expression, to make itself again one with the Infinite?

Obviously the first step to be taken towards unity with the Infinite is to free oneself as far as possible from this world. Suicide is useless as a means to this end, because the soul would in that case merely leave one bodily habitation for another—it would be merely a temporary physical relief, and not a permanent spiritual one. For the soul to be reunited with the universe we must quit this world, not only bodily, but, what is all-important, spiritually as well; and we can do this only by crushing down and overcoming all the desires that attach us, so to speak, to this world. Among these desires or attractions are of course power, wealth, good food and drink, fine clothes, and the pleasures of sex. These things we must all renounce. Hence we find Bhartrihari deprecating the world and the pleasures to be found in it—pleasures which he refers to as illusions—and telling us instead that the proper example to follow is that of the ascetic who lives in a mountain-cave or in the forest, and is content with little, whether garments, food, or drink. His book is by no means a long one, but nevertheless this principle is impressed upon us over and over again. Practically the whole of the Vairagya Sataka is one long glorification of the life of the ascetic, and an appeal to us—at times almost pathetic in its intensity—to give up the pleasures of the world for something better and more lasting. By meditation we become pure, and the more we concentrate our mind on Brahma the less we shall feel the attractions of the world, the more merit we shall acquire, and all the sooner consequently shall we fit ourselves for the supreme bliss.

Nothing is ever carried out to its logical

conclusion. It is obvious that if every unit in Indian society had become an ascetic, the magnificent hierarchy in the social order would have become a chaos, there would have been no one to attend to the fields or the herds, and there would have been no one even to supply the begging ascetic with the few alms he required. There did, indeed, come a time in the later history of Brahminism when there was a superabundance of ascetics, but human nature soon restored the normal balance. One effect, however, these religious principles did have, and that was to develop a contemplative mind in practically every Hindu, developing at the same time a peculiar calmness, accompanied nevertheless by a strong will power; a joint phenomenon which has always puzzled Westerners unacquainted with the bases of Indian thought. It is hardly necessary to say, however, that very different meanings may be attached to meditation, and what may be good meditative qualities in one mind may not be so in another. The question having been posed, "How can we become one with the Infinite?" the answers were not long in being given. What, perhaps, will strike the European as significant is the exceedingly minute manner in which all the processes of the mind have been analysed in India, together with all the effects produced on the mind by external things. Hardly any intellectual process has been left unaccounted for, and every possible shade of subtle meaning has been covered by a word. There is one expression to indicate the relationship existing between water and ice, and another to indicate the relationship existing between cloth as cloth and the same cloth made up into garments. These distinctions have perhaps been carried to their greatest extreme in that system of Indian philosophy known as the Nyaya, which has often been called the Hindu system of logic.

This Nyaya system of philosophy which has just been referred to is one of the so-called six orthodox systems—orthodox, not in that they agree on the nature or even the existence of God, but in the sense that they acknowledge more or less implicitly the authority of the Vedic writings. I have said elsewhere [1] that wherever we find a religious

[1] "The Religions and Philosophies of the East." (T. Werner Laurie.)

system well developed and capable of influencing almost every branch of even the everyday life of a nation, we find that as a general rule there is comparatively little room or necessity for a supplementary system of philosophy. It is approximately correct to say that the principles of Hindu religion are laid down in the sacred writings known as the Vedas, and that the six orthodox systems of Indian philosophy really amount in the end to little more than commentaries on the Vedas. Three of these "systems" indeed so closely resemble the other three that they may be described in pairs: (1) Mimamsa and Vedanta, (2) Sankhya and Yoga, and (3) Nyaya and Vaisehika.

It is true there are critics who hold that the Mimamsa is not, strictly speaking, a philosophy at all; but if we are going to omit the Mimamsa system from this list, we may as well leave out the other five systems also. Mimamsa—or rather Purva-Mimamsa, i.e. preliminary inquiry—is an attempt to systematise the principles which should be applied to the interpretation of Scripture, i.e. to the interpretation of the Vedas. We know this in Europe by the shorter title of exegesis. Apparently the Mimamsa philosophy dates from the second or third century of our era, and its reputed founder was one Jaimini, a sort of Indian Thomas Aquinas. The name of the second system, Vedanta, means "end of the Veda," and the alternative name for it of Uttara-Mimamsa, meaning "later inquiry," serves to describe it concisely. It sets forth at considerable length the process by which all things arose from Brahman, to which the soul is later on destined to return.

The third, or Sankhya system, is ascribed to Kapila, and represents what may, for the sake of convenience, be called the materialistic side of Indian philosophy. Sankhyaists ascribe the origin of the earth to a material first cause devoid of intelligence, from which the universe has been developed by a process of unconscious evolution. It will thus be seen that this third system of Indian philosophy has something in common with the older school of English evolutionists.

To the twenty-four principles laid down by the Sankhyaists, the adherents of the fourth or Yoga system add a twenty-fifth: "Nirguna purusha," i.e. the man, or rather the self, without attributes. This principle presupposes evolution based on some theistic principle, and on this account the Yoga is occasionally referred to as the theistic or Sesvara Sankhya.

The fifth and sixth systems differ essentially from one another in so few points that they are usually studied together. Nyaya, which literally translated means method or rule, is chiefly noteworthy for its complicated dialectics. The Vaisehika system is so called from its main principle, viz. that each separate atom (visesha) possesses its own individuality, and that the cosmos has been formed from an agglomeration of these atoms. This last system is a late development—it probably dates from the fifth century of our era—and it is interesting, but perhaps not very profitable, to compare the Indian atomic system as set forth in it with the atomic theory enunciated by Lucretius.

But no account of Indian philosophy, however elementary, would be complete without mention of one of the most remarkable books in literature, philosophy or religion, the "Bhagavad-Gita." This work, although written at an earlier date than the treatises on some of the six philosophical systems already mentioned, nevertheless includes principles common to them all. It is read by all creeds, castes, and classes of Hindus, and is of great importance in that it forms the basis of Hinduism as we know it at the present day—modern Hinduism may be summed up as a corrupt form of the ancient Vedism, influenced to some extent, although not very greatly, by the principles of the Buddhists. Bhagavad-Gita means "the song of the adored one," or, as it has perhaps been more accurately translated, "the divine lay." The hero or god of the book is Krishna, and the term Bhagavad-Gita or "adored one" is applied to him when he is identified with the Deity. We thus get the expression Krishnaism, which is often used to indicate the faith outlined in the "Bhagavad-Gita." This book nominally forms a part of the well-known Indian epic poem, the "Mahabharata"; but there is little connection between it and the other poems that go to make up that long epic—it is as if a chapter from the New Testament had unexpectedly found its way into the

Iliad. There is therefore some ground for believing, as most modern critics do, that the " Bhagavad-Gita " was simply added to the " Mahabharata " at a later date to give it the authority of antiquity and of divine inspiration. Probably the book appeared in a written form about the first century of our era, and there are many resemblances between it and the New Testament. It is beyond the scope of this Introduction to say which borrowed from the other, and I have already referred to the matter elsewhere. It will be sufficient for our purpose to say that it is much more likely that the New Testament writers borrowed from the " Bhagavad-Gita " than vice versa. As an instance of a resemblance between the two scriptural works a quotation or two may be given. Krishna says (ix. 27) " whatever thou doest; whatever thou eatest; whatever thou sacrificest; whatever thou givest away; whatever mortification thou mayest perform : do all as if to me." With this compare (1 Cor. x. 31) " whether therefore ye eat or drink, or whatsoever ye do, do all to the glory of God." Krishna says again : " Be not sorrowful; from all thy sins I will deliver thee": while in Matthew ix. 2 we read, "Be of good cheer; thy sins be forgiven thee." Let me add just one further dual quotation, in which the resemblance is, if possible, even more striking: in describing Heaven Krishna says of it that it is a place "in which neither sun nor moon need shine, for all the lustre it possesses is mine." The Heaven described in Revelation xxi. 23 is a city which "had no need of the sun, neither of the moon to shine in it, for the glory of God did lighten it."

The main theme of the "Mahabharata" being the war between the Indian tribes of the Kurus and the Pandus, the author of the "Bhagavad-Gita" in order that his poem might appear to form an integral part of the great epic, begins it with a description of the battle-field and the warriors. Long colloquies take place among the leaders of both sides in order that the reader may be made familiar with the somewhat complicated series of births, deaths, marriages, and intermarriages leading up to the main subject. There is, we may note in passing, still another analogy with the New Testament in these preliminaries, for some Indian Herod is described as having put to death all the first-born in a certain district. After this the two chief personages of the book are introduced, viz. Krishna and his disciple, Arjuna. Their subsequent dialogues develop for us their conception of the Supreme Deity, Krishna himself being, to describe him with approximate correctness, the god turned man who created the world. These dialogues may be summarised thus :—

Krishna is the Supreme God; he is superior to the other deities as well as Brahma, Vishnu, and Siva : furthermore he is "the only existence, the only real substance of all things." "I am the Cause of the production and destruction of the entire universe." "Nothing superior to me exists." "I am the origin of all gods, the great lord of the world without beginning."

The world is not a creation, but was produced by Krishna from his own nature (prakriti). He says : "All things exist in me. Supported by my material essence, I caused this entire system of existing things to emanate again and again, without any power of their own, by the power of this material essence. When a devotee recognises the individual essence of everything to be comprehended in one, and to be only an emanation from it, he then attains to the supreme spirit. Earth, Water, Fire, Wind, Ether, Heart, Intellect, and Egoism : into these eight components is my nature (prakriti) divided. This nature is an inferior one; but learn my superior nature, other than this, of a vital kind, by means of which this universe is sustained. Understand that all things are produced from this latter or higher nature." When it is completely developed, however, we find that the doctrine in addition to the eight component parts mentioned above includes fifteen others, the inferior nature being designated as avyakta, or non-developed matter, which is changed into vyakta, or developed matter, by the superior nature.

Man, again, is composed of an eternal, immortal soul which is an emanation from Krishna's superior nature, and of a mortal and perishable body derived from Krishna's inferior nature. The soul is subject to transmigration from body to body, until it is finally absorbed into Krishna's essence. This principle of transmigration is common both to Buddhism and to Brahminism, and of course Krishna's essence corresponds to the Vedic Brahman or to the Buddhistic Nirvana. As this latter word is by now fairly well known to Western readers, I have not scrupled to employ it occasionally in this translation of Bhartrihari, where the text would perhaps strictly call for some other but equivalent expression.

Reverting to the "Bhagavad-Gita" we are reminded that the only real existence is to be found in the Spirit, which is eternal. What we call matter does not exist at all. Matter is merely the delusion of Maya, the mystic power by which Krishna the supreme god has created a transitory world, which *appears* to be, but *is* not. "Krishna" is indestructible; "as a man abandons worn-out clothes, and dons new ones, so the soul leaves worn-out bodies, and enters other new ones."

Prakriti is composed of three qualities, (gunas) goodness, passion, and ignorance, (sattwa, rajas, and tamas), and the soul, being one with nature, comes under their influence. Hence the qualities referred to unite the soul with illusion and bring about transmigration.

Krishna, again, is responsible for all our actions, whether they are good or evil, for " all qualities (gunas), whether goodness (sattwa), passion (rajas), or ignorance in darkness (tamas), proceed from me." Krishna, we are likewise told, instituted the four castes according to the proportion of natural qualities and actions. The Brahmin excels in goodness, the Kshattriya in goodness and passion; the Vaishya in passion and ignorance, and the Sudra in ignorance alone. The " actions " of the first consist in knowledge, prayer, inspiration, and self-control, of the second sovereignty and the protection of the people, of the third commerce and agriculture, and of the fourth servitude.

I have previously referred to the fact that at one stage in Indian society the wish of everybody to become an ascetic almost upset the balance of the social order for a time. The exhortations in the " Bhagavad-Gita " had no little influence in restoring the balance, for " Krishna " emphasises the fact that it is impossible for any man to live without action of some sort, and he imposes upon all the castes the obligation of performing the duties laid down for them, while at the same time renouncing the world as much as they can. In order that this may be accomplished, of course, the passions must be subdued, and certain rules are given to show how this may be done. "A devotee should always exercise himself, remaining in seclusion and solitude, restraining his thoughts without indulging hopes and without possessions, keeping a couch for himself in an undefiled spot, not too lofty or too low. Then, fixing his heart on the Supreme Being, restraining his thoughts, senses, and actions, he should practise devotion for the purification of his soul. Holding his body, head, and neck, all even and immovable, firmly seated, regarding only the tip of his nose and not looking round in different directions, the devotee should remain quiet with passionless soul, free from anxiety and intent on me (Krishna) . . . Hear my supreme words, most sacred of all. Thou art very much beloved of me, and therefore I will tell thee what is good. Place thy affections on me, worship me, sacrifice to me, and reverence me. Seek me as thy refuge, and I will deliver thee from all sin."

As we might expect, Pantheism is an

essential doctrine of Krishnaism. All things are emanations from God or Krishna, and, therefore, no matter what things may be worshipped, he is worshipped in them.

When we have thus summarised the "Bhagavad-Gita," we have also summarised, as I have previously intimated, many principles common to the "Bhagavad-Gita" and the six orthodox philosophical systems already mentioned. The distinctions and further details need not concern us long.

In the investigation of truth the Indian philosopher works from within outwards: we begin with the ego, and not with the non-ego; with the noumenon, and not with the phenomenon. The ego and the non-ego are, however, related to one another, for it is impossible to gain a complete knowledge of the one without some knowledge of the other. If we admit that there is an outer physical world apart altogether from its cognition by the ego, we must also admit that it is impossible to prove the existence of this world until the ego is illuminated.

The Yogis, who fall into a deep sleep (sushupti) or into a profound trance (samadhi), will tell us that when they lose consciousness of the ego, they lose consciousness of the world at the same time, and that they do not begin to perceive the world again until they are once more conscious of their ego. The conclusion is thus arrived at that the " I " is the more important : consciousness of the " I " precedes the consciousness of the outer world, and we must therefore work from the ego outwards. The non-ego does not exist as something which is entirely independent of the ego, but is merely another aspect of it. Hence the non-ego is merged with the ego itself into " atman," which word may be variously translated as spirit, breath, or soul—i.e. the vital spark that pervades every created thing. At other times " atman " may mean the inmost nature of man and things, when the word becomes practically a synonym for idânta, which corresponds in a great measure to the mediaeval philosophic expression quiddity, and might occasionally be translated self. By a slight expansion of the meaning " atman " came to be used to represent the paramatman or the soul of the world. It is necessary thus to speak at some little length of " atman " because, next to the neuter

Brahman, it is perhaps the most important word connected with the Vedic religion.

It is the philosophical aspect of this religion which we find exemplified in the Vedic writings and in the commentaries upon them. The Vedas (veda may be roughly translated "knowledge") are also known as sruti, i.e. revelations—in other words, the revelations of the universal Brahman or "atman" to the rishis, or priests. The collections (sanhitas) of the sacred writings or "mantras" comprise:—(1) The Rig-Veda, (2) the Saman or Samaveda, (3) the Yajush or Yajurveda, (4) the Artharvan or Atharvaveda. To each of these textbooks or manuals of religion is attached a series of prose works (Brahmanas) the aim of which is to explain the text-books and the nature of the sacrificial rites mentioned in them. In some cases further commentaries are added, the Aranyakas and the Upanishads. The Aranyakas do little more than supplement the Brahmanas in a few points of little interest to Europeans, but the Upanishads are of greater value to us, since in them we find the fruits of early Indian speculation on the problems of the universe. The Saman and the Yajush, dealing mainly with matters of ritual, and containing many quotations from the Rig-Veda, are of small importance to all but Hindu theologians.

It is largely on the Upanishads that the six orthodox systems of Hindu philosophy are based, and of these six systems it will, I think, be generally agreed that the Vedanta is in nearly every respect the most important. Anyone, however, desirous of investigating the Vedic Philosophy very thoroughly may find the other "systems" of considerable value. Nyaya, the logical philosophy already referred to, lays down sixteen padarthas, or "topics," into which knowledge is divided. Through Nyaya the student learns to reason syllogistically and to deal with fallacies and false premises to an even better degree, perhaps, than Gil Blas at Salamanca.

Kapila's system of philosophy, i.e. the Sankhya, is based on numbers and ascribes considerable importance to evolution, while the Yoga, or system of union, ascribed to Patanjali, shows us how to reach the profound state of trance known as Samadhi, how to control the mind and the reason, and how to reach Kaivalya, or a state of bliss resembling the Buddhistic nirvana, by separating purusha (self) from prakriti (nature).

From this it will be observed that these various philosophical systems, however great may be their intrinsic value, are relatively of minor importance when considered in conjunction with the Vedanta. I do not propose in this place to go thoroughly into this noteworthy system, for space would not permit of it. It will, I think, be sufficient for the reader's purpose to know the main outlines of it, and these outlines have already been set forth above; for the importance of "atman," Brahman, and the transmigration has already been sufficiently emphasised, and these are among the main principles of the Vedanta philosophy. The complete Vedanta doctrine for philosophical purposes is summed up in two phrases used in the Upanishads: "Ekam Evadvitiyam," "Verily one without a second," and "Tat tvam asi"—"Thou art that." What is meant by Tat here is understood to be Brahman as the cause of the world, while Tvam would appear to represent "atman" in all its shades of meanings—in other words, we come back to the proposition that the self and the world are united, are one, that the ego and the non-ego are indissolubly bound.

Max Müller points out that this solution of the riddle of the world goes far beyond European ideas, because the Vedanta conception of what was the supreme cause of the universe went beyond their conception of what was meant by God. "Prajapati," their God in this sense, was, in their eyes, only one manifestation of the supreme cause, that is, of Brahma, but as Brahma was phenomenal, the cause of everything, of the all in all, it followed that man was likewise merely a phenomenon of Brahman. So far as mere substance went, therefore, creature and creator were equal, if not identical. The Tat, however, was something superior even to the creating deity; it was some kind of divine essence which is manifested, not only in man, but also in gods. When, however, Brahman ceases to be a neuter and becomes a masculine deity under the name of Brahma, he desires to know something about the details of the universe, and for this purpose he is assumed to divide himself into many. When he has thus divided himself, that part of the prakriti which contains the "atman" is called avidta or nescience and the other part of the prakriti, i.e. the part forming the cosmos, is known as the Maya. Maya is usually understood to mean illusion, and this may be taken as its definite secondary signification; but primarily Maya meant the power to create, and it was applied especially to the magic powers that enabled a god or a man to conceal his own personality by creating asomatous beings, incorporeal spirits which, although leading to no change in his own identity, nevertheless resembled him. At a late period in the development of the Vedanta philosophy, the theory was put forward that Brahma was a great magician exercising an eternal force or shakti of magic. By this force he was said to have created the phenomenal universe, simply as an illusive *corpus* of himself. To this later Vedantists added the proposition that that which we call the world of phenomena was not a tangible form of something whose appearance was illusory but it was itself a radical illusion. Maya possesses two powers; in the first place it may cause the absolute self to appear limited or it may conjure up, so to speak, before the eyes of the self illusory visions of the details of the universe as if they really existed outside the self, and could be seen by the self. No doubt we all remember Plato and the shadows on the wall.

As for the details of the Vedanta teaching to be found in the Upanishads I propose to follow Professor Max Müller's excellent example by giving a few extracts from actual works of the old philosophy. I have chosen mine from a little book by Mr L. D. Barnett, of the British Museum, entitled "Some sayings from the Upanishads," not merely because his own extracts are sufficiently condensed, though ample for the purpose, but because his translations are of a very high order.

There was one Svetaketu, Sruni's son. To him his father spake saying, "Svetaketu, go walk the Brahma way. Truly there is none of our stock beloved who is unlearned and a Brahmin by birth only."

Twelve years old was he when he went in; and when he was four-and-twenty years old he had read all the Vedas, and came home swollen of soul, deeming himself learned, and haughty. To him his father spake saying, "Svetaketu, thou art swollen of soul deeming thyself learned and haughty; but, beloved, hast thou sought the lore whereby that which is not heard is heard, that which is not thought is thought, that which is not understood is understood?"

"Nay, my lord," said he, "how may this lore be?"

"As by one clod of clay, beloved, all things that are of clay must be understood, their several shapes being but an holdfast of speech, and their name being in truth clay. As by one copper toy, beloved, all things that are of copper may be understood, their several shapes being but an holdfast of speech, and their name being in truth copper; as by one iron nail knife, beloved, all things that are of iron may be understood, their several shapes being but an holdfast of speech, and their name being in truth iron; so is this lore, beloved."

"Indeed, my lords knew not of this. Had they known it how should they not have spoken to me thereof? But now let my lord tell it to me."

"Be it so, beloved," said he.

"Being was This in the beginning, beloved. One with naught beside. Now some say that Not-Being was This in the beginning. One with naught beside, and from this Not-Being was born Being. But how in sooth may it be so, beloved?" Thus he spake. "How from Not-Being may Being be born. Nay, Being was This in the beginning, beloved, one with naught beside.

"It thought in itself 'I will be many, I will beget offspring.' It brought forth Heat.

"The Heat thought in itself 'I will be many, I will beget offspring.' It brought forth Water. Therefore whensoever a man sorrows or sweats from heat ariseth thereupon water.

"The Water thought in itself 'I will be many, I will beget offspring.' It brought forth food. Therefore whensoever it raineth there is very much food. From water ariseth thereupon food for eating.

"Food eaten is sundered in three. The thickest stock thereof becometh dung, the middling flesh, the thinnest Mind. Water drunk is sundered in three. The thickest stock thereof becometh the body's water, the middling blood, and the thinnest Breath. Heat eaten is sundered in three. The thickest stock thereof becometh bone, the middling marrow, the thinnest Speech.

"So Mind, beloved, is of Food, Breath is of Water, Speech is of Heat."

"Let my lord teach me further."

"Be it so, beloved," said he.

"When milk is churned, beloved, the thinness thereof riseth up; it becometh butter. So indeed when food is eaten, beloved, the thinness thereof riseth up; it becometh Mind. When water is drunk, beloved, the thinness thereof riseth up, it becometh Breath. When Heat is eaten, beloved, the thinness thereof riseth up, it becometh Speech. So Mind, beloved, is of Food, Breath is of Water, Speech is of Heat.

"Man is of sixteen sixteenth-deals, beloved. For fifteen days eat not, but drink Water as listeth thee. Breath is of water, once drunk it may not be severed."

For fifteen days he ate not, and then drew nigh unto him saying, "What shall I say, my lord?"

"The Rik-spells, beloved, the Yajus-spells, the Sama-spells."

"Nay, my lord," said he, "they come not to my mind."

"If of a great piled fire, beloved," said he, "there should be left but one coal as big as a glow-worm, it would not then burn much withal; and so, beloved, of thy sixteen sixteenth-deals but one-sixteenth deal can be left, and with that now thou has not any thought of the Vedas. Eat thou. Then shalt thou learn of me."

He ate, and then drew near to him. Whatsoever he asked him he answered all. And thus he spake to him. "If of a great piled fire, beloved, there should be left one coal as big as a glow-worm, and one should set it afire by laying grass upon it, it would then burn much withal; and so, beloved, of thy sixteen sixteenth-deals but one hath been left, and it hath been set afire by laying food upon it. With that now thou hast thought of the Vedas. So Mind, beloved, is of Food, Breath is of Water, Speech is of Heat."

This of him he learned, yea, learned.

. . . . . .

"Bring from yonder a fig."

"Lo, my lord."

"Break it."

"It is broken, my lord."

"What seest thou in it?"

"Lo, little seeds, as one may say, my lord."

"Now break one of them."

"It is broken, my lord."

"What seest thou in it."

"Naught whatsoever my lord."

Then he said, "Of that thinness which thou beholdest not, beloved, ariseth this fig-tree which is so great. Have faith, beloved. In this thinness hath this All its essence. It is the True. It is the Self. Thou art it, Svetaketu."

. . . .

Brahma in sooth is this All. It hath therein its beginning, end, and breath, so one should worship it in stillness.

Now man in sooth is made of will. As is Man's will in this world, so doth he become on going hence. Will shall he frame.

Made of Mind, bodied of breath, revealed in radiance, true of purpose, ethereal of soul, all working, all loving, all smelling, all tasting, grasping this All, speaking naught, heeding naught: this, my self, within my heart is tinier than a rice corn or a barley corn or a mustard seed or a canary seed or the pulp of a canary seed. This my self within my heart is greater than earth, greater than sky, greater than heaven, greater than these worlds.

All working, all loving, all smelling, all tasting, grasping this All, speaking naught, heeding naught, this is my self within.

This is Brahma, to him shall I win on going

hence. He that hath this thought hath indeed no doubt.

. . . .

I think that these selections, together with the remarks I have previously made on the Vedas, will give the reader an adequate conception of the principles of Indian philosophy. Some few difficulties may be encountered by the apparent incoherence, or, as some people may be inclined to say, the uselessness of many of Bhartrihari's aphorisms. They all, however, have their use and their place in this book, and even the most apparently useless among them points out some definite goal to some section, however small, of our vast Indian population.

One or two more or less excellent translations of Bhartrihari have already appeared in India, and more than twenty years ago the Rev. B. Hale Wortham prepared an English translation for Trübner's "Oriental Series." In nearly all these cases, however, the Sringa Sataka was omitted. It is true that this particular section of the book deals with eroticism and many passages would not be suitable for publication in English without some modification. Still, it is unwise to omit one-third of the book, and I have accordingly included it here, merely drawing the reader's attention to the fact that there are many passages in the Song of Solomon to which as much objection may be taken as to some of the aphorisms of Bhartrihari.

As for the author himself, particulars of his life are very scanty. Beyond saying that he "flourished" about the eighth or ninth century A.D. we cannot even assign a date to him. Many authorities, however, give plausible reasons for thinking that he lived as early as the second century. It may be taken for granted that he was the son of King Gandhavasen of Malwa. Bhartrihari, the story goes, duly succeeded to the throne and led for seven years an indolent and licentious existence in spite of the warnings and entreaties of his half-brother Vicrama. We are told, however, that Bhartrihari one day found out that he was being deceived by his favourite wife, whereupon his life suddenly changed and he sought relief in devotion and meditation. The aphorisms, according to the best authorities, sum up his devotional life. This is the most probable theory, although other authorities hold that

Bhartrihari merely collected many sayings from the lips of wise men, sifted them, chose the best, and handed them on for the use of posterity. Each Sataka or "century" is supposed to consist of one hundred aphorisms, but the texts vary a little and a few supplementary "slokas," or verses, ascribed to Bhartrihari add to the number. Such as they are, good and bad, they have been of spiritual service to tens of thousands on their way to join

> "The innumerable caravan, which moves
> To that mysterious realm, where each shall take
> His chamber in the silent halls of death."

J. M. KENNEDY.

THE WISE SAYINGS OF BHARTRIHARI

CHAPTER I

THE NITA SATAKA[1]

1. Hail to the Almighty Power who cannot be defined in terms of Time or Space—who is Infinite: pure intellect incarnate; who is peace and glory, and whose unique essence is self-knowledge.

2. I believed that one woman was devoted to me, but she is now attracted by another man, and another man takes pleasure in her, while a second woman interests herself in me. Curses on them both, and on the god of love, and on the other woman, and on myself.

3. The fundamentally ignorant man is easily led, and the wise man still more easily; but not even the Almighty Himself can exercise any influence on the smatterer.

[1] Niti=moral principles, moral philosophy: ethics.

4. A man may tear the pearl from between the teeth of the crocodile; he may steer his ship over the roughest seas; he may twine a serpent round his brow like a laurel; but he cannot convince a foolish and stubborn opponent.

5. A man may squeeze oil from sand; he may slake his thirst from the well in a mirage; he may even obtain possession of a hare's horn;[1] but he cannot convince a foolish and stubborn opponent.

6. To try to lead wicked men into virtuous ways by the mere use of soft words is as futile as tethering an elephant with the fibre of a young lotus, as futile as the attempt to cut a diamond with a piece of wood, as futile as trying to sweeten the salt sea with a drop of honey.

7. God has given to man a cloak whereby he can conceal his ignorance; and in this cloak he can enwrap himself at any moment, for it always lies near his hand. This cloak is Silence: an ornament peculiarly fitted for an ignorant man in the company of wise men.

[1] A próverbial expression for something that does not exist.

8. When I had acquired but a little knowledge my pride in it made me as blind as its passion does an elephant—my head was swollen, and in my ignorance I thought I knew everything. But I soon met with wise men who were acquainted with many different kinds of wisdom, and my pride disappeared as if it had been only a fever.

9. A dog will eat with delight the most noisome and decaying bones, and will pay no attention even if the ruler of the gods stands before him—and in like manner a mean man takes no heed of the worthlessness of his belongings.

10. The River Ganges descends from on high upon the head of Siva, from the head of Siva to the mountain, and from the summit of the mountain to the earth. Its fall is always lower and lower, and in this way it resembles the fall of any man in whose mind judgment no longer finds a place.

11. Water will put out fire; a parasol will ward off the sun's rays: a sharp prong will guide the wild elephant, or a stick the ox and ass: yea, sickness can be cured by the physicians; and there are antidotes even for

poisons. The shastras prescribe remedies for everything, but there is none for curing the fool.

12. The man who cannot appreciate music and literature is exactly like the lower animals, even though he may not possess horns and a tail: though he eat not grass he yet lives a life precisely like that of the kine.

13. Those who possess not wisdom, contrition, generosity, knowledge, good temper, virtue, or uprightness, may take the shape of men while they live among us, but they travel through life nevertheless like beasts that encumber the ground.

14. It is better to roam among the mountains with the wild beasts than to live in palaces with the fool.

In Praise of Wisdom

15. When it happens that sages, whose words are enriched with beautiful thoughts from the shastras, and who convey their sacred learning to their pupils, are compelled to dwell in poverty, then the princes of whom they are subjects must be accused of foolishness, and these sages, however poor they may be, are the real rulers of the country. If those

whose business it is to examine jewels are so careless in their methods as to lower the value of the stones, should we not be right in condemning them?

16. O princes, cast away your pride in the presence of those who are rich in the inward treasury of wisdom: they cannot be robbed by thieves, but their treasure, which is continually increasing, becomes even larger when they share it with the needy, and it will not perish even at the end of the world! Who can compare with the wise?

17. Despise not the wise men who have reached a knowledge of the Truth. They cannot be influenced by money, for wealth to them is but as grass. An elephant blind with passion cannot be bound by the stalk of a water-lily.

18. Brahma in his anger may prevent the swan from gratifying its natural instincts in the lotus-bed where it lives, but he cannot remove its faculty of separating milk from water.[1]

19. Bracelets do not set off a man's appearance, nor do strings of pearls as

[1] A faculty attributed to the swan in ancient Indian literature.

pure and clear as the moon; nor yet bathing, perfumes, flowers, and carefully dressed hair. Nothing adorns a man but perfect eloquence. Jewels may perish, but the adornment of eloquence lasts for ever.

20. Wisdom is truly the most beautiful ornament that a man can possess. It is a thing of value, and must be carefully watched, for it brings with it food, fame, and blessings. It is the lord of lords. Wisdom is like a friend to the man who travels in distant countries. It is honoured by kings even more than riches, and the man who lacks wisdom is but an animal.

21. If a man have patience, why should he need armour? But if he have anger in his heart, what other enemy need he fear? If he have knowledge, why should he need fire to consume evil? If he live among evil-disposed people, why need he be afraid of serpents? If he possess perfect wisdom, why should he strive for wealth? If he be modest, why should he require ornaments? If the muses are his friends, why should he need a kingdom?

22. Show yourself well-disposed towards relatives and liberal to your inferiors. Hate

all things evil; love the good; be obedient to the king; honour the wise. Be firm with your enemies and respectful to old men; be shrewd in your dealings with women. These are qualities that will enable the man who acts upon them to prosper in the world.

23. Social intercourse with the wise takes away all dullness of mind, exalts the intellect, and imbues our words with the spirit of truth. What indeed will it not do for men?

24. Honour and glory to those sages who are scholarly and skilful poets! They need not fear that their fame will wither away or perish.

25. A virtuous son, a loving wife, a kind master, a devoted friend, an affectionate kinsman, a mind free from care, a handsome figure, lasting riches, lips that speak wisdom—such are the gifts that Hari, the giver of bounties, bestows upon the man who has found favour in his sight.

26. Refrain from taking the life or coveting the wealth of another. Telling the truth, moderate liberality in proportion to one's wealth, abstinence from pleasure-seeking among other men's wives, crushing the spirit of covetousness, reverence for the

priesthood, and compassion towards all—these are the ways of happiness, ways that break no defined rules, and that are taught in all the shastras.

27. The man whose mind is of a low order does not take the slightest trouble to pursue wisdom owing to his fear of the difficulties with which he may meet; and, if he does make any attempt, he stops as soon as he encounters an obstacle. On the other hand, the man of superior mind never ceases to pursue when once he has begun, no matter what hindrances he may meet with on the way.

28. Righteousness must be loved, and evil avoided, even on pain of death. There must be no intercourse with wicked men, and a poor man, however friendly, must not be asked for an alms. Dignity must be retained, even in adversity, and the doctrines inculcated by good and great men must be adhered to, even though the attempt to do so is as difficult as trying to stand on the edge of a sword.

In Praise of Firmness

29. The lion may be overpowered by hunger, and his strong frame weakened by

old age; he may lie in a state of misery and at the point of death; his majestic appearance may have departed from him, and his life may be slowly ebbing away; yet his one desire is to swallow at a mouthful the brow of the noble elephant that he has crushed in pieces. How could he, the mightiest of all living things, feed merely upon the withered grass!

30. The dog finds the dirty little fleshless bone of some ox, and over this he will rejoice, even though it may not satisfy his hunger; but the lion scornfully passes by the jackal, and rushes upon the elephant. In like manner, the man of firm mind, no matter what a condition of distress he may be in, seeks that which is most in accordance with his natural disposition.

31. The dog falls prostrate at the feet of anyone who gives him food, wagging his tail and opening wide his mouth; but the elephant remains unmoved in such circumstances, and will not eat until he is coaxed with flattering words.

32. What man is not born again when he passes from one earth to another by transmigration? But we must hold that the only

man who is truly born is he by whose birth his family attains to dignity.

33. There are but two uses for a bouquet of flowers and for a wise man : they may be exalted [on the head], or left to wither in the forest.

34. Although we think a great deal of the half-dozen planets of which Vrihaspati is the head, nevertheless Rahu, whose power and strength are great, does not attack them. The god of the demons, though there is nothing of him left but the head, devours in his course only the lords of the day and of the night.[1]

35. Shesha supports all the worlds on the flat surface of his serpent-like head, and he himself is borne on the back of the King of Tortoises, who is kept without difficulty in his dwelling-place at the bottom of the sea. Ah ! with what ease are these great marvels performed by the mighty.

36. The son of Himalaya would have acted with much greater nobleness if he had

[1] The immortal Rahu having offended the gods, Vishnu cut off his head. Rahu was then placed among the stars, and when an eclipse occurred he was said to have swallowed the sun and moon.

allowed the angry Indra to cut off his wings with the flaming thunderbolt, instead of seeking a refuge by throwing himself into the sea, when his father was suffering in misfortune.[1]

37. The sun-stone, though not sensitive, kindles into light when the rays of the sun fall upon it: and how then can we expect a powerful man to tolerate an injury inflicted by another?

38. A lion, however young, will rush upon the infuriated elephant; but the energy of the man of noble mind arises from his natural temperament, and not merely from his youth.

In Praise of Riches

39. Our nobility of birth may pass away; our virtues may fall into decay: our moral character may perish as if thrown over a precipice:[2] our family may be burnt to ashes, and a thunderbolt may dash away our power like an enemy: let us keep a firm grip on our money, for without this the whole assembly of virtues are but as blades of grass.

[1] This refers to a fable in the Ramayana, v. 8.

[2] A play on a word meaning "stone" and another very like it meaning "character," "disposition."

40. We may behold a man's senses and observe them to be unchanged; we may see precisely the same gestures and an unimpaired intellect, together with the same voice. Let a man remain exactly as he was in all other respects, he nevertheless becomes quite a different person when the warmth that wealth has afforded him is taken away. This is truly wonderful!

41. Let a man be wealthy, and he shall be quite wise, learned in the sacred writings and of good birth; virtuous, handsome and eloquent. Gold attracts all the virtues to itself.

42. A king is brought to ruin by evil counsellors; an ascetic by moving in society: a child by being spoilt: a priest by not studying the sacred writings: a family by the wicked behaviour of children: good manners by bad habits: modesty by strong drink: agriculture by neglect: affection by absence from one's household: friendship by want of love: possessions by careless management, and money by waste and prodigality.

43. Giving, spending, and losing are three ways by which the amount of one's wealth is

lessened, and the man who neither gives nor spends may yet be ruined by the third way open to him.

44. A jewel is cut away by the stone when it is polished; a victor in warfare is killed by arms : the elephant is weakened by passion : the islands in a river become arid in the autumn : the moon wanes, and young women become languid through sexual passion, though their beauty does not deteriorate : and in like manner noble men who have got rid of a certain proportion of their wealth by bestowing it on the needy still remain illustrious.

45. When a man is starving with hunger, he longs for a few grains of rice, but when his appetite has been satiated, he regards the whole earth as but a handful of grass. Similarly do objects appear great or small according to the condition of their owners : it is only the change in the fortune of men that makes things seem greater or smaller.

46. If, O King, you would then enjoy this earth, which is as fruitful as a cow, tend it as carefully as you would a calf. The earth, like a bounteous tree, will bring forth fruits

year by year if it is constantly and carefully cultivated.[1]

47. The behaviour of a king is uncertain as the behaviour of a courtesan. At one time it is false and at another true; now harsh and now agreeable: now cruel and now merciful: sometimes generous and sometimes greedy: either squandering money recklessly, or piling it up like a miser.

48. Authority, renown, the care of the Brahmins, generosity, feasting and the guarding of friends: what profit comes to them who serve kings if these six blessings have not fallen to their lot?

49. Whatsoever destiny has prescribed for every man, that shall be his portion, whether wealth or poverty. He may be poor in the desert, but he shall be no better off even if he live on Mount Meru.[2] Let your nature be constant, and become not miserable by envying the rich. The pitcher holds the same quantity of water, whether it be filled from the well or the depths of the ocean.

50. "Who does not know that thou, O

[1] In Indian literature the earth is often compared to a cow.

[2] The Indian Olympus: also applied to any wealthy place or district.

cloud, art the only support of the chataka,[1] and why, O most bountiful cloud, dost thou wait for our cry of distress?"

51. "Ah, my dearest chataka, hearken attentively to my words. There are many clouds in the heavens, but they do not all resemble one another: some pour their waters on the earth, while others thunder and give forth no rain."

Do not demean yourself by asking favours of any chance person with whom you may meet.

Of Evil Men

52. Cruelty; senseless quarrelling; the desire for the money or the wife of another: envy of the good and of one's own relatives: these are the characteristics of wicked men.

53. Even when the wicked man is learned, he should be avoided. Should we fear a snake the less if it were ornamented with jewels?

54. In many ways we find that evil-disposed persons misrepresent the virtues of the good. The virtue of the moderate man is called dullness: the rigid ascetic is looked upon as arrogant: the pure-minded man is

[1] A bird which is supposed to live only on raindrops.

said to be deceitful: the hero is termed pitiless and the wise man contemptible. The polite man is looked upon as servile and the noble man as proud. The eloquent man is referred to as a chatterer, and freedom from amorous passion is described as weakness.

55. If a man be covetous, what worse vice can he have? What sin is worse than slandering? Why should the cheerful man stand in need of penances? Why should the pure-minded man require a sacred bathing-place? What virtue is higher than generosity? If a man possess greatness of mind, what further adornment should he require? If a man be learned, why should he stand in need of the company of others? And if a man is overtaken by disgrace, why need he be afraid of death?

56. There are seven thorns in my side: the moon cast into obscurity by daylight: a woman who has grown old: a pond without water-lilies: a handsome man who talks foolishly: a prince who gives himself up entirely to money: a good man who is always in distress, and an evil man who is admitted to the king's Court.

57. A wrathful king has no friends. If

the priest who offers up the sacrifice touches the sacred fire, then he will be burnt by it.

58. The laws regulating behaviour are indeed difficult to learn, and can hardly be mastered, even by the ascetic. The man who wishes to be respectfully silent is liable to be looked upon as dumb : the man who talks agreeably may be thought too forward. If a man stands near at hand, he may be regarded as troublesome, and if he stand far off, people may call him cold-hearted. The patient man may be branded as timid, and the impetuous man is looked upon as ill-bred.

59. How is it possible to delight in the company of a low and abandoned man whose evil ways are all too obvious : whose wicked deeds are the consequence of former births : who dislikes virtue, and lives only by chance?

60. The friendships which are formed between good and evil men differ in kind. The friendship of the good man may at the beginning be as faint and dim as the first appearance of the morning light, but it continually increases, while the friendship of the evil man is as great at the beginning

as the light of the noonday sun, but it soon dies away like the twilight of the evening.

61. Deer, fish and men of virtue, who have need only of grass, water and peace in this world, are deliberately pursued by huntsmen, fishermen and envious people.

Of the Character of the Good

62. A desire for the society of the good: love for the virtues of others: reverence for priests and teachers: diligence in acquiring wisdom: love for their wives: fear of the world's reproaches: reverence for Siva: self-control and no acquaintance with evil men—wherever we find men with virtues like these, they are invariably held in high esteem.

63. Firmness in adversity; self-control in prosperity: eloquence in debate: valour in war: desire for glory: knowledge of the sacred writings: such are the characteristics of the virtuous.

64. Private generosity; ungrudged hospitality to strangers: abstinence from speaking in public about one's good deeds: openly proclaiming the benefits received from others: humility in prosperity, and

respect for one's fellows—this is a sacred doctrine taught by the good, though adherence to it may be as difficult as the attempt to stand on the edge of a sword.

65. There are sufficient inward adornments adequate for the man of noble mind without the necessity for a more evident display—liberality for his hand; reverence towards the priesthood for his head; true speech for his mouth: power for his arms; happiness for his heart; and the holy Vedas, properly understood, for his ears.

66. In prosperity the heart of the wise man is as soft and pliable as the lotus; but in adversity it is as firm as the imperishable mountain rock.

67. Though water will not remain on a hot iron, it shines with the beauty of a pearl if it lies on a lotus leaf: yea, let a drop of water fall under a favourable star into an oyster on the ocean bed, and it forthwith becomes a pearl. So also is the nature of men, good, tolerable or bad, according to the society in which they live and move.

68. Three things are the reward of virtue —the son who pleases his father by his good deeds; the wife whose sole concern is her

husband's good, and the friend who remains unchanged in prosperity and in adversity.

69. Who cannot but respect and reverence those whose admirable behaviour is exhibited in many different ways; as for example in those who are ennobled by humility; those who exhibit their own virtues by speaking only of the virtues of others: those who even in their own business always bear in mind the interests of others: and those who hate the evil speaker, or the lips that continually utter harsh and impatient words.

Of Liberality

70. Trees when laden with fruit are bowed down, and the clouds when pregnant with fresh rain hang near the earth: and in like manner good men are not unduly exalted by prosperity. This is the natural disposition of the liberal man.

71. The ears of men like these are ornamented by hearing the revelation of divine wisdom, and not with ear-rings; their hands are adorned by liberality rather than by bracelets and rings: and their bodies shine by the doing of good unto others, and

not by being anointed with the oil of sandal-wood.

72. A good man flees from evil and pursues the good: he does not utter that which ought to be kept secret: he does not conceal his virtues: he does not neglect his friends in adversity: and he gives according to his means. And these, the wise men tell us, are the characteristics of a good friend.

73. The sun opens up the lotuses; the moon brightens the beds of the water-lilies: and the cloud pours down its rain unasked. And in like manner those people who are naturally liberal are continually occupied in bestowing benefits on their fellow-creatures.

74. Good men devote their attention to benefiting others without thinking of themselves. Ordinary men benefit others, but they do not at the same time forget their own interests. Those men are demons who destroy the good of another for their own profit. But what can we call those who wilfully destroy the possessions of another?

75. Milk which has been mixed with water conveys to the water its own natural

qualities. The water sees the milk becoming hot, and immediately offers itself up as its sacrifice in the fire. The milk also wished to boil over into the fire, but, having observed its friend's distress, it remains mingled with the water and rushes into the fire with it. To this we may compare the friendship of the good.

76. The ocean bears the sleep of Vishnu, and the mountains also take refuge in the ocean after their flight from the demons; and, in addition to this, a great submarine fire continually devours the ocean's depths. What cannot the ocean endure!

77. How do the good behave: they curb their amorous desires; are patient in all circumstances; are not deceived by illusion; do not long for what is evil; speak the truth; hold fast that which is good; seek the company of virtuous men; honour the wise; become reconciled even with their enemies; conceal their own virtues; take care of their good name; and show themselves merciful to those in adversity.

78. How few noble spirits there are whose thoughts, speech, and actions are, so to speak, impregnated with nectar, by whom

countless blessings are bestowed upon the three worlds: who exalt even the slightest virtues of another to the height of a mountain, and whose hearts are continually overflowing!

79. What profit or advantage is there in Meru, the mountain of gold, or the hill of silver, where the trees grow up like their companions, and undergo no change? We reverence the hills of Malaya, for after coming into contact with them, the bitter nimba, the karaya, and the trophis aspera, become themselves like the sandal-tree.

In Praise of Constancy

80. Men of firm mind never rest until they have carried out to the end the task they have set themselves to do, just as the gods did not rest until they had gained possession of the nectar: for they were not turned aside from their search by pearls of great price, or by fear of dreadful poison.

81. At one time a man may lie on the hard earth, and at another he may sleep on a couch: at one time he may make his meals of herbs, and at another of boiled rice; at one time he may wear the meanest rags, and

at another the most magnificent robes. But the man of firm mind, who is thinking only of the task he has undertaken, does not look upon either state as one of pleasure or pain.

82. A man's natural disposition, from which his virtues arise, is his most precious ornament—courtesy of a noble man; gentleness of speech of a hero; calmness of knowledge, and reverence of sacred learning. The highest ornament of wealth is liberality towards worthy objects: the highest ornament of the ascetic is abstinence from wrath: the highest ornament of princes is mercy: and the highest ornament of justice freedom from corruption.

83. Those who are skilful in reading character may be inclined to praise or to blame the constant man; fortune may be kind to him or may neglect him; and he may die to-morrow or not for ten thousand years. But in spite of all this, nothing can make him turn aside from the path of righteousness.

The Power of Fate

84. One night a rat fell into the jaws of a serpent whose body had been forced into a basket, and who was half-dead with hunger.

Revived by his meal, the serpent managed to struggle out, but, as a stronger animal was close at hand, he perished by the same fate as the rat. My friends, be content with your lot! The success or failure of men lies in the hands of fate alone.

85. Though a ball fall to the ground, it rises again when struck by the hand. So too the misfortunes of good men are not often lasting.

86. Mankind's great enemy is idleness. There is no friend like energy, and if you cultivate that you will never fail.

87. When the tree is cut down, it may grow again, and the moon that wanes, waxes once more. Thus do wise men reflect; and, though they may be distressed, they are not overwhelmed by misfortune.

88. Though Indra was guided by Vrihaspati, and armed with the thunderbolt: though the gods themselves were his soldiers, and Vishnu his ally: though he had Svarga as his citadel, and the elephant Airasvata as his charger; yet he was defeated. How irresistible is the power of fate, and how vain the efforts of mankind!

89. Discernment is the consequence of

human actions, and is brought about by deeds performed in another life. This must be carefully taken into account by the sage who gives heed to all things.

90. The bald-headed man was scorched by the fierce rays of the sun, and when he was looking for a shady place, fate guided him to a palm-tree. While he was resting there, the fruit of the tree fell on his head with a loud crash, and broke it. Wherever the unfortunate man goes he usually meets with disaster.

91. When I see the sun and moon delivered up by the eclipse to the power of the demon: when I perceive the bonds that fasten a serpent or an elephant, or when I perceive a wise man dwelling in poverty, the thought forces itself on me—"How mighty is the power of fate!"

92. Fate first creates a good man—a stronghold of virtue—and then in an instant brings about his ruin. How unreasoning is fate!

93. It is not the fault of the springtime that the leafless tree does not bring forth leaves; it is not the fault of the sun that the owl cannot see by daylight; and it is not the

fault of the cloud that its rain does not drop into the mouth of the cuckoo. Who can interfere with what fate has written on the foreheads of us all?

In Praise of Action

94. We worship the gods, but are not they too controlled by fate? Fate must be worshipped, for it is the only giver of rewards to mankind in accordance with the acts which have been performed in the previous existence. But the fruit of those acts depends upon the acts themselves, so why then should we worship either the gods or fate? Let us rather worship those works which it is in the power of fate to control.

95. Through fate Brahma was compelled to work like some artificer in the interior of his egg: through fate Vishnu had to pass through ten extremely difficult reincarnations: through fate Siva was constrained to lead the life of a beggar, carrying a skull in his hands as a pot: and through fate the sun is forced to make his daily round in the heavens. To works therefore let us give our reverence.

96. What will bring fruit to a man as to a tree in its season? Not beauty: not greatness of family: not strength of character: not learning: not careful service; but merit alone: merit resulting from penances in a former state.

97. Let a man wander in the forests: let him take part in war, or let him be in the midst of a fire or amongst enemies or in the ocean or on top of a high mountain: let him be asleep or mad or surrounded by difficulties: the good actions he has performed in a former life will nevertheless profit him.

98. O wise man, make a regular practice of cultivating divine virtue; for that makes wicked men good, foolish men wise: enemies well-disposed, and invisible things visible. Divine virtue will in an instant turn poison into honey, and will bestow upon you the fruit of your actions.

O virtuous man, do not vainly spend thy labour on painfully acquiring powerful gifts!

99. When the wise man begins his actions, he looks carefully to the end of them, in order that through them he may become freed

from successive births and reach Nirvana. Actions carried out with too much haste are like an arrow that pierces the heart.

100. The man who does not act circumspectly in the world of action and keep a constant eye on his state in another life is even as one who cooks the lees of sesame over a sandal-wood fire in a pot of lapis lazuli, or as one who uses a golden plough in preparation for cultivating swallow-wort, or as one who cuts down a camphor grove to fence in a field of coarse grain.

101. A man may plunge into the deep waters of the ocean: he may ascend to the summit of Mount Meru: he may conquer his enemies or devote himself to commerce: he may plough the earth and devote himself to all learning and all art; and he may even travel on the wings of a bird from one end of the heavens to the other: but he shall nevertheless suffer whatever fate may have prescribed for him on earth.

102. All men worship the virtuous man whose deeds in his former existence were righteous: for him the terrible wood becomes a magnificent city and the whole world is as if filled with jewels.

Miscellaneous Aphorisms

103. What is of the greatest advantage? The companionship of the good. What is the worst thing in the world? The society of wicked men. What is the greatest possible loss? Failure to perform one's duty. Where is the greatest peace to be found? In truth and righteousness. Who is the noblest hero? The man who subdues his senses. Who is best loved? The faithful wife. What is wealth? Knowledge. What is the most perfect happiness? Staying at home. What is royalty? The power to command.

104. The man with intelligence, like the jasmine flower, has two alternatives to choose from: he may blossom and flourish in the sight of the world or wither away in the desert.

105. The world is differently adorned in different places—by poor men whose words are of little value: by rich men whose words are treated with respect: by those husbands who are satisfied with their own wives, and by men who abstain from passing censure on others.

106. The lighted end of a torch may be

turned towards the ground, but the flame still points upwards : the constant man does not lose his virtue in misfortune.

107. The arrows shot from the bow of love cannot pierce the mind of the constant man, neither is he consumed by the fire of anger, nor snared by the net of greed : he is the lord of the three worlds.

108. The mighty earth, when trodden on by the feet of a single hero, is illuminated by his glory as by the rays of the sun.

109. The constancy of the constant man makes the savage things in nature turn into the most gentle. By the power of constancy fire becomes as water : the ocean as a rivulet : Mount Meru as a small stone : a lion as harmless as an antelope : a savage animal as a bunch of flowers, and poison is even changed into honey.

110. Honourable men may turn away from life and happiness, but, as they are bent upon truth, they do not cast off their truthfulness. Truthfulness, which is the origin of modesty and of all the virtues, follows them wherever they go : it makes them pure in heart, and is as dear to them as their own mother.

111. A sour heart; a face hardened with inward pride and a nature as difficult to penetrate as the narrowest of mountain passes —these things are known to be characteristic of women: their mind is known by the wise to be as changeable as the drop of dew on the lotus leaf. Faults develop in a woman as she grows up, exactly as poisonous branches sprout from the creeper.

112. It does not matter whether a brave man who is killed in the thick of the fight obtains heaven or victory: he will in any case be held in the highest glory by both armies, and this is the object of the man who desires fame.

113. Of all the great marvels that I have ever seen, the boar and Rahu are the greatest.[1] The former supported the round earth on his tusks which were dripping with water; and the other, who has only a head, swallows his enemy and then lets him go free again.

114. The earth is bounded by the ocean, and the ocean extends in length but a thousand yojanas; the sun again pursues a

[1] The god Prajapati assumed the form of a boar when lifting the earth out of the waters. Rahu: v. note to aphorism 34.

certain definite path through the sky; whence it follows that all these things are bounded by certain definite limits. Nothing exceeds them in greatness but the intelligence of wise men, for the intelligence of wise men has no limits.

115. There is one god, Vishnu or Siva: one friend, a king or an ascetic: one dwelling, in a town or in the country; and one wife, handsome or ugly.

116. The earth shakes and trembles, even though it is supported on the king serpent, on the great mountains, or on the tortoise; but whatever has been promised by pure-minded men never fails, even though ages may have passed away.

117. If the tortoise is over-burdened by the weight of the earth, why does he not cast it off? If the sun becomes fatigued as he pursues his journey, why does he not stand still? When a noble man takes note of these examples, he is ashamed to fail in his promises, and faithfully keeps his word. In this manner are vows adhered to in the household of a good man.

118. If a man is satisfied with food, he may be looked upon as subject to the world,

even as a drum gives forth an agreeable sound when its surface is covered with flour.[1]

119. Men of low and mean minds take an interest only in their own affairs; but men of noble mind take a particular interest in the affairs of others. The great fire on the ocean bed absorbs the waters of the sea to slake its insatiable thirst, and the rain-cloud replenishes itself from the ocean, that it may relieve the drought of the arid earth.

120. The Minister of State, like the poet, is never free from trouble: he collects revenue as the poet collects thoughts from afar. He disregards false reports as the poet disregards vulgar language; both devote themselves to pleasing the assemblies of the good, and, with the expenditure of much toil and labour, the statesman makes a name as a poet makes a verse, by conforming to the thoughts of the world.

121. Whatever fate has prescribed for each man in this life, that shall be his portion, great or small. Rain pours from the cloud day by day, filling all things, but only a

[1] That is, a man praises his patron when supplied with food, as a drum was heard better when flour was spread over the leather that formed one side of it.

few tiny drops may fall into the mouth of the chataka.

122. Wise men must be reverenced, even when we may not think the advice they give us suitable or desirable. The ordinary conversation of such men is like what we read in the Holy Scriptures.

123. A good man may tumble, but if he does, he comes to earth like a ball, and rises again; whereas the ignoble man falls like a heavy lump of clay.

124. If fate decreed that the world were ever to become deprived of lotuses, might we expect to see the swan scratching in the dust-heap like a cock?

125. Elephants blind with passion or heavy with sleep may stand at the gate: horses decorated with golden ornaments may gallop speedily backwards and forwards, and their owner may be awakened by the sound of drums, shells, cymbals, fifes and lutes; and all this state—a state like that of the king of the gods—is the outward reward of religious merit gained in a former existence.

126. Perfect indeed is the joy of those men whose minds are awakened to the happiness of contentment, but unceasing is

the desire of those who cannot resist their greed for riches. For whose sake did fate create Mount Meru full of wealth? Mount Meru pleases me not, though it is filled with abundance of gold and silver, because it is satisfied with itself alone.

127. There are three qualities, each perfect in its own sphere as the result of its natural disposition: the red colour of the lotus; the consideration for others shown by the good; and the want of respect shown by the wicked.

128. Fidelity in keeping promises is the noblest quality among men; leanness is the best characteristic of a female elephant; and wisdom and patience are best suited to a Brahmin. Every creature, in other words, shows to best advantage when adorned with its own particular ornament.

129. It is better to slip from the highest summit of an elevated mountain and be dashed to pieces on the rocks below—it is better that our hand should be bitten by the poisonous fangs of the most dreadful serpent—it is better that we should fall into a roaring fire, than that our piety should fail us.

CHAPTER II

THE VAIRAGYA SATAKA [1]

Of Renunciation

1. Hail to the Almighty Power, who cannot be defined in terms of time or space—who is Infinite; who is Peace and Glory, and whose unique essence is self-knowledge.

2. Wise men are consumed with jealousy, the mighty are injured by pride, the minds of some are led astray by ignorance, wherefore it happens that the eloquent sayings of the learned are left to fall into neglect.

3. When I cast my eyes upon the world, I see no advantage in any action. The consequences of good actions inspire me with fear when I reflect upon them, for the pleasures resulting from the long practice of the highest virtues prevent men from attain-

[1] Vairagya = lack of desire for the world; renunciation.

ing to Nirvana, since they are afterwards attracted by objects appealing to the senses.

4. I have dug up the earth in the search for treasure : I have smelted ores : I have travelled across the sea : I have with great effort calmed the wrath of kings. I have spent my nights in burial-grounds, and I have striven hard to acquire knowledge of religion ; but all my strivings have been fruitless. Desire ! wilt thou not leave me ?

5. I have wandered over strange and rugged lands, but without profit ; I have freed myself from my pride of family : I have carried out valueless tasks : I have put away my self-respect, and have eaten like the crow in the house of a stranger ; but yet, O Desire ! thou becomest more and more powerful : always with evil inclinations and never satisfied.

6. I have endured the abuse of wicked men in the hope of gain ; I have smothered my tears and forced myself to laugh, though my heart was sad and weary : I have controlled my feelings, and I have bowed down before fools. O fond Desire, how much further dost thou wish to lead me ?

7. Day by day a portion of our life glides

away from us with the rising and setting of the sun, and we think our business of so much importance that we can pay no attention to flight of time. We perceive that birth, pain, and old age end in death, and yet we are not afraid. We are, so to speak, intoxicated—intoxicated by the want of infatuation.

8. Though a man might expect to be refused, and might even stammer, when making his request, he would beg for alms if he saw his wife perishing from hunger, her garments worn and ragged, and her children clinging to her crying, with pinched unhappy faces; but yet such a man would not beg merely to satisfy his own wants.

9. Pleasure has no longer any attraction for us; the world no longer respects us: our contemporaries have died away one by one; the friends whom we love as we love ourselves will shortly follow: we hobble along leaning on a stick, and our eyes gradually become dim. Alas! these are signs that our body has been subdued, and that it is trembling at the approach of death.

10. It is the will of the Almighty that the serpents shall gather their food from the air

without effort to themselves, and without injury to others, while the cattle have been created to eat blades of grass and to lie on the ground. Precisely the same method of living has been decreed for men who pass through this world with subdued senses: men who endeavour to live in this way continually bring themselves nearer and nearer to perfection.

11. We have not meditated on the Almighty Being who at last puts an end to all our reincarnations: we have not as the result of our righteousness been able to open for ourselves the gate leading to Svarga:[1] we have not gratified our sexual appetites with a woman, even in imagination. If our life has been spent in this way, we have but destroyed the tree of youth that came to us from our mother, even as if we had hewn it down with an axe.

12. We have not gained any pleasure, but pleasure has made us captive. We have not endeavoured to practise penance, but on the other hand we have suffered pain when pursuing the joys of this world. Time never grows old, but our own lives pass away.

[1] The paradise of sensual enjoyments.

13. We have pardoned the injuries done unto us, not because we wish to show forgiveness, but because we are unable to avenge them; we have cast away the pleasures of home, not because we were willing to abandon them, but because they were beyond our reach; we have had to suffer pain from cold winds, but we have shrunk from doing penance on account of the pain it would have caused us; we have meditated day and night on the art of getting rich, but we have never meditated on the Supreme Being; and although we have performed all the acts recommended by wise men we have derived no profit from them.

14. My face is wrinkled and my hair is turning grey; my limbs are weak, and only desire is strong within me.

15. The same portion of the sky that forms a circle round the moon by night also forms a circle round the sun by day. How great is the labour of both!

16. The objects of the senses, no matter how long they may be in our company, must one day pass away from us, but there is a difference between our separating ourselves from them, and not giving them up. If they

leave us, we shall be smitten with pain and grief difficult to parallel, but if we leave them of our own free-will, our reward will be enduring peace and happiness

The Power of Desire

17. All desire comes to an end in a man when he gains self-control by discriminating between what is wise and what is useless; but desire gradually becomes more and more violent when one has got into contact with the panoply of royalty—in consequence of this even the mighty Indra himself, the lord of the winds, is a prey to desire; for he is wretched because of the desire he feels for his position as a royal personage, a position that age has made null and void.

18. A miserable, tailless dog, worn out, lame, deaf, covered with sores, perishing from hunger, and with a fragment of a broken pot tied round his neck, still pursues his mate. Even that which is already dead is destroyed by love.

19. A man may get his food by begging, and the tasteless scraps he receives may be sufficient for only one meal; his bed may be the cold, hard ground: he may have no one

to attend to him but himself, and age may have worn his clothes away to rags which are ready to fall to pieces. Alas! even then objects of the senses retain their hold on him.

20. The beautiful features of a woman are praised by the poets—her breasts are compared to pots of gold: her face to the shining moon, and her hips to the forehead of an elephant: nevertheless the beauty of a woman merits no praise.

21. Ignorance will lead the moth to fly into the flame of the candle, and the fish may nibble at a piece of meat fastened to a hook without being aware of the bait prepared for them; but we men who know thoroughly the many traps and snares that fortune has set for us nevertheless refuse to give up our desires. Ah, in what a forest of error do we wander!

22. The fibre of the lotus is sufficient food for us. We want nothing to drink but water. We may lie on the bare ground, and we may be clothed in the meanest of garments. I do not approve of the wicked behaviour of evil men whose senses are led astray by the lust of gold.

23. In former times the created world was ruled by wise men, and afterwards by others. It was thrown aside like a bundle of straw after they had conquered it, and even now heroes rule the fourteen divisions of the world.[1] To what, then, can we ascribe the frenzied desire that some men possess for a few cities?

24. You are a king, and I belong to the band of spiritual teachers whom the world honours for their wisdom. Your riches are celebrated, and my renown is celebrated by the poets. So then, O bestower of blessings, there is no very great interval between us. Thou hast turned thy face away from me, and nevertheless I desire not thy favour.

25. Innumerable rulers have quarrelled with one another, and still continue to quarrel, for the possession of worldly enjoyments, and kings still retain a feeling of pride for their dominions. The foolishness of those who own the earth leads them to manifest unmistakable delight in the acquirement of the most minute particle, while they ought, on the contrary, to exhibit the most profound sorrow.

[1] That is, the entire earth.

26. What is the earth but a lump of clay surrounded by the vast ocean? Kings have conquered it in battle after battle, and have divided it among themselves. These evil, contemptible men may or may not show themselves generous—neither characteristic on their part need surprise us. But shame on those mean men who would beg alms from them.

27. I am no actor; I am no courtesan; I am no singer; I am no clown, and I am not a beautiful woman: what then have I to do with the palaces of kings?

28. At one time men availed themselves of wisdom to obtain relief for earthly pains and troubles, and afterwards they used wisdom as a means for the attainment of pleasure. But now, alas, it is clear that men care nothing for the sacred learning, and therefore every day that passes sees them further estranged from it.

29. That man alone is born truly great whose white skull exalted on high is worn as an ornament by Siva, the enemy of Kama. The only true honours being those conferred by Siva, what can be the meaning of this pride and magnificence now displayed by

kings who are so greatly worshipped by other men, and think only of their own royal lives?

30. Thou art the king of wealth, and I of speech: thou art a hero in war, while my talents are seen by the manner in which I can conquer the haughty and arrogant by the power of my eloquence; men bow down to thee, but they come and hearken unto my words that their minds may become purified. And if thou, O king, hast no desire for me, my desire for thee is still less.

31. When the knowledge I possessed amounted to but little, I was puffed up with pride like an elephant blinded by passion, and I thought there was nothing I did not know. But when I learned many things from the sages, my foolishness became evident to me, and I was freed from my mad excitement. [*Cf.* Niti Sataka, aphorism No. 8.]

Indifference

32. Time is passed by, whiled away without difficulty in the agreeable society of beautiful women; our long wanderings in incarnation after incarnation have fatigued us and worn us out. We repose on the banks

of Siva's river, and call to him with frenzied cries, "Siva! Siva! Siva!"

33. When our honour has departed and our wealth is lost; when our desires have left us and we have profited nothing by them; when our relatives are dead and our friends vanished away, and when our youth has slipped from us bit by bit: there is then only one thing left for a wise man—a mountain cave where he can dwell in peace and quiet, a cave whose rocks are purified by the waters of the Ganges.

34. Why, O my heart, dost thou try from day to day to secure the good graces of others, and yet all in vain? If thou wert only purified, surely all thy desires would be gratified, and thou wouldst not seek the favours of other men, since inwardly thou wouldst be at rest.

35. In our periods of health we are alarmed by the fear of disease; in the pride we take in our family by the fear of a sudden fall; in wealth by the fear of a grasping ruler; in honour, by the fear of degradation; in power by the fear of enemies; in beauty by the fear of old age; in our knowledge of the Scriptures by the fear of controversy; in

virtue by the fear of evil; and in our body by the fear of death. Everything on earth gives cause for fear, and the only freedom from fear is to be found in the renunciation of all desire.

36. These lives of ours are as unstable as the drop of water on the lotus leaf, and yet what do we not strive to do for their sake? We sin even when we are brazenly boasting of our own virtues in the presence of those wealthy men whose minds have become petrified by the intoxicating power of riches.

37. All hail to the power of Time! The pleasures of the town, the glories of the monarch with his crowds of courtiers, his ministers who stand respectfully before him, his women with faces as beautiful as the shining moon, the crowds of haughty noblemen, the poets and the writers—all these are carried away on the stream of time and eventually become but a memory.

38. The previous generations who gave us birth have long since passed away, and even those with whom we grew up exist now only as a memory, while by the approach of death we ourselves are become like trees growing on the sandy bank of a river.

39. In the dwelling where there were once many there is now only one; where there was only one there were afterwards many, and then again but one. In such a way are day and night dashed hither and thither by Kala and Kali,[1] as if they were pieces of dice, and thus too do Kala and Kali play with men on the chess-board of this world as if they were chessmen.

40. Shall we abandon the world, dwell beside the divine river, and lead a life of penance? Or shall we rather seek the society of virtuous women? Or shall we study the multitudinous Scriptures, the poetry of which is even as nectar? We cannot tell what we shall do, for the life of a man endures but the twinkling of an eye.

41. Men, to their disgrace, are now living on the sustenance they have obtained from others. What then has happened? Are there no longer retreats among the Himalayas where the vidyadharas live among the imperishable rocks cooled by the spray from the water of the Ganges?

42. When shall we lie at rest on the

[1] The male and female incarnations of the destructive principle.

margin of the divine river whose banks of sand shine with a dazzling whiteness under the light of the moon? And when shall we, when the nights are calm and still, satiated with the world, utter cries of "Siva! Siva! Siva!" while the tears flow from our eyes?

43. Mahadeva is the god we worship, and this river is the divine river; those caves are the abode of Hari. Kala too is our friend, and the rules of life which we follow bring us freedom from humiliation. So what more need I say on this point?

44. The same as aphorism No. 10 of the Niti Sataka.

45. Desire resembles a river; its waters are like men's wishes, blown hither and thither by the waves of passion. Love takes the place of the crocodiles, and the birds that soar over the surface of the stream are like the doubts that beset men's minds. The tree of firmness that grows on the bank is carried away by the flood; the whirlpools of error are difficult to navigate, and the steep banks of the river are like unto the troubles of our life. Thus ascetics who, with purified hearts, have succeeded in crossing the river are possessed with unbounded joy.

46. When we look upon the ceaseless changing of the three worlds, the passion concealed within us, violently attracted by the objects of the senses, ceases to cross the horizon of our eyes or to enter into the radius of our ears; for we have crushed down the objects of the senses that bring about desire in us, and we now have them, so to speak, bound down by devotion, even as the elephant, attracted by his mate, is kept from her by being tethered to a post.

47. Once upon a time the days seemed long to me when my heart was sorely wounded through asking favours from the rich, and yet again the days seemed all too short for me when I sought to carry out all my worldly desires and ends. But now as a philosopher I sit on a hard stone in a cave on the mountain-side, and time and again in the course of my meditations I often laugh when I think of my former life.

48. We have not acquired stainless wisdom; we have not obtained wealth; we have not treated our elders with the respect due to them, and we have not even dreamed of love. If we have lived a life of this kind, then our existence has been like that of the

crow, which looks greedily on the food of others.

49. Let all our wealth depart from us, and then with tender hearts and recollecting how activity in the world leads to deeds of evil, we shall sit in some sacred grove with the calm rays of the autumn moon shining upon us, and there pass our nights at the foot of Siva, occupied only in meditation.

50. I am satisfied with the meanest of cloth; thou delightest in thy splendour, and yet my contentment is equal to yours. Poor indeed is the man whose desires are boundless, but who that is satisfied with what he possesses can be called either rich or poor?

51. Freedom from toil whenever we feel inclined to be free from it; food obtained without a stain on our honour; friendship with men of noble spirits, and a mind undisturbed by contact with the outside world—all these things result from the noblest vow of tranquillity. Although I have given careful thought to this matter, I know not by what strict penance this perfect state may be reached.

52. Their hand serves them as a cup; their food is obtained by begging; the pure

expanse of the heavens serves them for a garment, and the earth is their couch. Those who are no longer attracted by the objects of the senses are fortunate if they have reached this stage of perfection. Content in their own minds, they cast away all action, casting away at the same time all the innumerable forms of pain which are inseparable from action.

53. Masters are hard to please; the whims of kings change from one thing to another with the swiftness of rapid horses; our desires are violent, and in our minds we aim high. But old age withers our bodies, and death puts an end to our existence. O my friends, for a wise man there can be no glory in this world but that which he gains from penance.

54. Amorous passion is like a flash of lightning in the cloud. Life itself is like the clouds which are torn in pieces by the storm, and the ardent desires of young men soon pass away. O wise men, ye who know how uncertain are human affairs, gain wisdom by meditating on the Supreme Being, for perfection soon results from continual contemplation.

55. A hungry man who is gifted with understanding will go from door to door through a sacred village, and will beg for alms where he sees the door-post blackened by the smoke of the sacrifices offered up by the priests who dwell there. He will bear before him his pot covered with white cloth, and he will not live in misery from day to day among families as wretched as himself.

56. "Are you a chandal? Are you a Brahmin? Are you a Sudra or an ascetic? Or a lord of devotion whose mind has been developed by meditating on the truth?" Ascetics, when loud-voiced men ask them questions like these experience neither pleasure nor irritation, but quietly pursue their way.

57. O my friend, fortunate indeed are they who have freed themselves from the shackles of this world, and from whose minds all desire for early objects, like the poison of a serpent, has passed away. People like these spend the night illumined by the clear rays of the autumn moon on the borders of the forest, thinking of nothing but their own good fortune.

58. Wander no longer with weary foot-

steps in the thickets of the senses. Rather find out that better way, which in a single instant will bring thee freedom from all trouble. Join thyself to the Supreme Being and abandon thy own state, which is as unstable as the waves of the sea. Take pleasure no more in transient earthly things. O my heart, be calm!

59. O my friend, nourish thyself on fruits and nuts and lie on the bare ground: let us arise and enter the forest clothed in new soft garments made from the bark of trees. There in that retreat we shall no longer hear the voices of those rich men whose minds are dulled with ignorance and whose very voices are troubled and unsteady as the result of the confusion of their minds.

60. O my friend, let the delusion with which thou wert beset be cleared away; pay thy devotions to the god of the moon-crest, who frees man from delusions. Let thy thought be fixed on the stream of the heavenly river; for what certainty is there in things earthly, in waves and bubbles or in the flashes of lightning or in women or in the tongues of flame or in serpents or in the onrushing waters of the stream?

61. If there are songs in front of you, skilful poets from the south on one side of you and dancing girls with tinkling ankles and pearls behind you; then, my friend, enjoy the pleasures of the senses which these things may afford you. But O my mind, if you have not these things, then plunge into devout meditation, freeing thyself from all thought.

62. O sages, pay no attention to women who are only pleasing on account of their beauty, and delight in whose society is but transitory. Seek rather the company of women who are merciful, agreeable and intelligent, for the beautiful forms of women ornamented with tinkling jewels will not profit you in Naraka.

63. This aphorism is identical with No. 26 of the Niti Sataka.

64. O our Mother Lakshmi, vouchsafe that I may not be filled with longing or the desire for pleasure! Now having purified myself with the vessel of leaves joined together, let me maintain my life by means of the barleycorn that I have received as alms.

65. Once upon a time you resembled me

in all things, as I did you. But our feelings towards one another have altered: how has it now come about that we have changed?

66. O woman, why dost thou dart beautiful glances at me from thy half-opened eyes? Stop! stop! Thy labour is in vain! I am no longer what I was; my youth has left me: I live in a forest, and am no longer infatuated. To me now the pleasures of this world are but as grass. [*Cf.* Sringa Sataka, aphorism No. 93.]

67. The eyes of this woman have stolen the beauty of the lotus, and with them she continually glances in my direction. What can she want? My love has left me, and I no longer feel the pangs of the cruel passion that leads to warm blood and fever. [*Cf.* Sringa Sataka, aphorism No. 94.]

68. Is it not agreeable to dwell in a palace; is it not pleasant to listen to songs, and is not the company of friends whom we love, as much as we love ourselves, delightful? Wise men nevertheless withdraw from all these things, and take refuge in the forest, looking upon them as the light of a lamp that burns with a flickering flame

through the draught caused by the wings of a wandering moth.

69. Why do you throw aside your self-respect and bow down to haughty men who have with trouble amassed a small fortune and look upon you with unutterable contempt? Are there no more roots growing in the caves? Have the mountain torrents now ceased to flow? Do the trees no longer bear fruit or has the bark out of which you can make your clothing withered where it grew?

70. The same as aphorism No. 41 of the Vairagya Sataka.

71. When the end of the present epoch at length comes, and Meru the most magnificent of mountains falls from its place; when the ocean, the abode of innumerable monsters, is dried up, and when the earth itself comes to an end: where shall we be able to find any home for the body—this body of ours, as unstable as a young elephant's ear?

72. O Siva! when shall I, whose drinking-cup is my hand, whose solitary garment is the sky, and who live a lonely and peaceful life free from desire and action, when shall I

at last attain to union with the Supreme Spirit?

73. You may have gained glory, and all your desires may have been accomplished: what further? Your feet may have been placed on the necks of your enemies: what further? You may have given all your wealth away to your friends: what further? You may live thousands of years: what further?

74. You may have been clothed in rags: what then? You may have worn magnificent silk garments: what then? You may have had only one wife: what then? You may have had innumerable horses, elephants, and attendants: what then? You may have enjoyed good food: what then? Or you may have eaten wretched food towards the end of the day: what then? What matters any one of these states, if you do not know the glory of the Supreme Being who destroys all evils?

75. You have worshipped Siva; you have lived in the fear of death and believed in re-birth in another state; you have severed yourself from the affection you bear to your own family; you have not been influenced

by love; you have lived in a forest far apart from man, and you have not been soiled by contact with the world. If you have spent your life in this way, free from all attachment to external things, then you possess Vairagya.

76. Give yourself up to meditation on the Supreme Being, who is eternal and who grows not old, increasing his authority by his own will. What profit can be drawn from the delusions of this world? If a man is really bent upon being united with the Supreme Spirit, all the power and pleasures afforded by the earth seem to him to be fitted only for men of narrow understanding.

77. O my mind, thou canst enter Patala, thou canst fly across the heavens and the earth in an instant of thought. How does it come about that thou dost not even accidentally meditate at any time on the Supreme Spirit, stainless, dwelling within himself? For in this way thou mightest become tranquil.

78. We are men lacking in intelligence, and we take it for granted that day and night go on indefinitely, consequently we take up our task day by day, and continue it where

we left off. Alas! ought we not to be ashamed of our folly? We put up with the pains of this world, while we are entirely given over to enjoying the same objects of the senses over and over again.

79. The wise man, glad in his heart because he has been freed from desire, lives as happily and peacefully as if he were the ruler of the universe. The earth to him is an agreeable couch; the arms of the creepers are his pillow; the pure sky is his canopy; the winds are his fan and the moon is his glowing lamp.

80. Any man who has acquired great power thinks even the overlordship of the universe an insipid thing. Seek not pleasure in the enjoyment arising from flattery, dress or feasting. The only pleasure which is supreme is eternal and continually increasing. That is the pleasure which you should endeavour to secure, for compared with its sweetness there is no pleasure in all the three worlds.

81. What profit can be drawn from the vedas or the smriti[1] or from the reading of the puranas or the tiresome shastras or even

[1] That which has been handed down by tradition.

in the innumerable and bewildering multitude of ceremonial actions that lead to a resting-place in the heavenly tabernacles? In comparison with that final fire which is to consume the creations of this wearying burden of sorrow which we know as existence —the fire that will in the end unite us with the Supreme Spirit—all else is but the mere bargaining of merchants.

82. Life is uncertain as the waves of the sea; the glory that envelopes our youth remains with us for a short time: wealth passes away like a flash of thought: all the pleasure the world can afford endures no longer than a gleam of lightning in the heavens. The ardent passion of the mistress you clasp in your arms will last but a short time. Give all your thoughts, therefore, to the Supreme Spirit; for you too must navigate the sea of life with all its fears and dangers.

83. Why should the wise man be anxious over a small portion of this world? Is the mighty sea ever agitated by the movements of the little fish?

84. When the blinding effects of love had filled me with ignorance the world seemed to

contain nothing for me but women. But now since my eyes have been anointed with the oil of discrimination, I can see all things clearly, and I look like the creator upon the three worlds.

85. Delightful indeed are the rays of the moon, delightful the grassy corners of the forest, delightful the company of friends whom we love, delightful too the writings of the poets and delightful the face of our loved one when shining through the tear-drops of rage. But when we allow ourselves to reflect on the uncertainty of these delights, who can care any more for them?

86. An ascetic is one who lives by begging, far away from the busy haunts of men. He is self-controlled and walks in the path of indifference. It makes no difference to him whether he receives or does not receive, whether he gives or does not give. His only garment is a torn cloak made up of rags cast away by other men. He has no pride and no self-consciousness: he is untroubled by desire and his only pleasure is rest and quietness.

87. O the Earth, my mother! O the Wind, my father! O Fire, my friend! O

Water, my wife! O Sky, my brother! I hail you all with my hands clasped. I am enveloped in glory through the merit I have acquired by my union with you. O, may I become part of the Supreme Spirit!

88. So long as the temple of the body is well and strong; so long as old age is still far in the distance; so long as the senses remain unimpaired, and so long as there is no diminution of life: precisely so long must the wise man make every effort to enter into eternal glory. What does it avail to dig a well when the house is on fire?

89. Alas, our youth has passed away from us unprofitably like a lamp set alight in an empty house. The knowledge which puts an end to the quarrels of disputants and which it is desirable for the thoroughly cultured man to have, has not been studied by us during the period we have spent on earth; our fame has not been exalted to the heavens by the sword-point that splits even the hard brow of the elephant, and we have not tasted the nectar on the lower lip of the soft mouth of our beloved one at the time of the rising of the moon.

90. In good men knowledge casts out

pride, but in others it leads to arrogance. In the same way a lonely dwelling enables ascetics to become freed from all attraction to the objects of the senses, but it leads to violent desire in those for whom it is unsuitable.

91. Our passions have gradually become weaker and weaker: our youth has turned into old age, and even the virtues in our own bodies have withered away because they are no longer recognised to be virtues. What remains for us to do? Omnipotent time is hastening on, and death is approaching to put an end to our lives. What is there for us but to throw ourselves at the feet of Siva? Other means of salvation there are none.

92. When a man's lips are parched he drinks water and finds it sweet to the taste. When hunger comes upon him he eats rice and vegetables. But he is in error if he thinks that the removal of the pain caused by hunger and thirst is a pleasure.

93. I will immerse my body, O Lord, in the waters of the Ganges; I will sacrifice to thee with unblemished fruits and flowers. I will meditate upon thee: I will sit on a rock

in a mountain cave and nourish myself on fruits with a quiet mind. I will revere the voice of my spiritual father. And when, O enemy of love, when lying at thy feet, shall I be freed from the pain of desire, and able to walk alone on the path of meditation?

94. Whom may we rightly call the over-lords of the earth: those who pay homage to any man? Those who are content to lie on a hard rock; who live in caves; who make their clothes from the bark of trees; whose only companions are the antelopes; whose food is the tender fruit; whose drink is water from the mountain stream and whose wife is wisdom.

95. Consider women as they sit showing every sign of extreme misery and of the pain resulting from the fever of distress. But what wise man would look at women in this condition, unless he felt merciful towards his unhappy family, so long as the Ganges was near at hand, the holy river from whose gleaming surface the sun's rays kiss the head of Siva, the river that furnishes us with food and drink, and with clothing made from the bark of the banyan-trees growing on its banks.

96. Alas, to what other towns can the sages resort if they leave Benares? For in the beautiful gardens of Benares the pleasures are innumerable, and penances of great difficulty are practised; a little torn piece of cloth is considered as a magnificent garment and there is no limit to the quantity of food that may be obtained by begging: even death itself in that place is like a festival.

97. " Our master sleeps; this is the hour when he takes his rest and you must not enter, for if he awakened and saw you he would be angry." Thus speak the keepers of the palace gates. But pass by them, and enter the temple of that master who rules the whole universe—that shrine that affords us boundless blessing, full of love and mercy, and where the coarse speech of the gate-keepers cannot be heard.

98. O my friend, relentless fate, like an omnipotent potter, puts the mind of man on the wheel of care as if it were a lump of clay, and makes it revolve—that wheel of care which moves ceaselessly amid all the innumerable evils of existence, inflicting itself upon men as if it were a scourge.

99. I can see no difference between Siva the master of the world and the slayer of Janu, and Vishnu the soul of the entire universe, consequently I worship the deity with the moon-crest.

100. I am well content with that divine voice which utters over my mind words that are sweeter than nectar and richer that ghee.[1] I am satisfied also with alms and clothing from the bark of trees, and I care nothing for wealth gained by becoming a slave to objects of the senses.

101. The ascetic may be clothed in ragged garments; he may beg his food; he may make his bed in the corner of a cemetery; he may no longer care for friend or foe; his dwelling may be lonely; but in spite of all these things he nevertheless lives in peace, rejoicing because all the intoxication resulting from pride has disappeared.

102. The various pleasures which may be met with in this world are every one ephemeral, so why then, O men, do you wander hither and thither, taking such trouble to pursue them? Let your soul free

[1] Sweet clarified butter—the word is well known to readers of Pilpay.

itself from the innumerable shackles of desire, and enter into the dwelling of peace which shall be its portion if you believe what I say unto you.

103. Blessed are they that live in a mountain cave and meditate on the glory of the Supreme Spirit. The birds of the air will come and perch fearlessly on their hands, and drink the tears of joy that flow from their eyes. As for us, however, our life quickly slips away while we are enjoying ourselves in the woods or by the river banks and devoting ourselves to the pleasures of this world.

104. Every living thing on earth is destined to perish. Youth passes into old age; happiness is destroyed by greed; peace of mind by glances shot from the eyes of beautiful women. Just men are slandered by the envious; serpents infest the forest, and kings themselves come to grief through their evil advisers. Not even the divine virtues themselves are permanent, so that everything in the world undergoes loss or damage in some form.

105. The health of men suffers through sickness, and when fortune has once left us,

we are overwhelmed by distresses which come in upon us as through an open door. Death indeed rules all things, for fate has decreed that nothing shall be permanent.

106. Alas! when everything is brought into the reckoning, what pleasure can be found in this world? Men have suffered pain in the narrow womb of their mother, and youth, when we have to separate from our beloved, is full of grief, while old age, since it exposes men to the contempt of women, is a thing of evil.

107. The full span of man's life is a hundred years: half is spent in night, and of the rest half is spent in childhood and old age. Labour, grief, separation and illness take up all that is left of us. What pleasure, then, can we find in the life of man, which is as unstable as the bubbles on the stream?

108. Men of pure minds, who are able to distinguish between the true and the false, are able to carry out difficult tasks by their communion with the Supreme Spirit, for they are able to cast away from them entirely the source of all pleasure, viz. worldly wealth. Where we are concerned, neither that which we formerly possessed nor that

which we have now really lies within our power. What we find it difficult to abandon is that which we only wish for in our minds.

109. Old age threatens our body like a tiger, and sickness finally carries it off. Life ebbs away like water from a cracked jar, and nevertheless man is able to lead a wicked existence in this world. And this is indeed wonderful.

110. The Creator makes a man a jewel, a man of virtue, an ornament to the whole earth—and then in a single instant he destroys him. Alas! what a lack of knowledge the Creator displays!

111. What innumerable evils are attached to old age! The body becomes bent with years; the steps grow more and more hesitating; the teeth fall out; the eyes become dim; deafness is more and more evident; saliva dribbles from the mouth; servants no longer obey orders; one's wife is not submissive, and even one's son becomes an enemy.

112. For a single instant one is a child, and for a single instant again one is a passionate youth. At one moment wealth lies about us in abundance, and the next it is no longer to be seen. A man reaches the end of his span

of life, and then with his limbs worn out by old age and covered with wrinkles, he enters the abode of death as an actor at the close of the play makes his exit behind the curtain.

113. It matters not whether a man wears a snake or a string of pearls; whether he is in the company of powerful enemies or powerful friends; whether he owns sparkling jewels, or is merely the possessor of a lump of clay; whether he reposes on flowers or on a stone; whether he is surrounded by fields of grass or by hosts of pretty women: this makes no difference to him at the time when, as he dwells in a sacred grove, he calls upon Siva.

114. What man finds the world filled with delight? Only he who has his passions under control, who is calm and content, and whose mind is never thrown off its balance.

115. Our final emancipation from the world is drawing near in the form of death, but yet we give no thought to it. We have lived through different stages of our life and have experienced calamity, happiness, adversity and dangers—what more can we add? Alas! what injuries have we not done ourselves over and over again.

116. The belly is as a pot which it is difficult to fill: it withers a man's virtue as the moon withers the lotus beds. It is like unto the thief who steals a purse; yea, it is even as a gleaming axe that hacks at the roots of the tree of virtue.

117. Let us eat the food we have begged; let the sky be our clothing; let the earth be our bed: why should we be slaves to cruel masters?

118. "O my friend, arise and bear the heavy burdens of poverty, and let me, overcome as I am with weariness, at length enjoy the repose that thou hast gained from death." Thus did the man who had lost his wealth address the corpse on its way to the graveyard, but the lifeless body remained silent, knowing that death is better than poverty.

119. The glory of Hara, who is glad because he is half man and half woman, and because his adored spouse thus forms part of his own being, is seen in men who are devoured by passion; but the same high deity, when freed from union with his wife, watches over those who are no longer subject to the pangs of passion. The man who is

confused by the almost unbearable poisoned arrows of love, cheated by Kama, can neither enjoy nor give up the objects of the senses.

120. At one moment women laugh and at another they weep, and in this way, although they are full of insincerity, they make men put their trust in them. Hence it comes about that the wise man avoids women as he would avoid a drinking-vessel used in a cemetery.

121. Let us pass our life at Benares living by the banks of the divine river, clad only in a single garment, and with our hands uplifted over our heads. Then let us cry in supplication, "O spouse of Gauri, Tripurahara, Sambhu, Trinayana, shower thy mercies upon us," and in the midst of our prayers we should find that days and years would pass by as if they were brief moments of time.

122. A firm bosom; sparkling eyes; a small mouth; curling hair, slow speech, and rounded hips are characteristics of a woman which are always praised. But when we neglect the surface we find that the internal characteristics corresponding to these are hardness of heart, shifty eyes, a deceitful face, insincerity and cunning. When we

bear in mind both the superficial and the inward characteristics of a woman, we must declare that the one who should possess them can be dear only to the beasts of the field.

123. Sometimes we may listen to music and singing; sometimes to weeping and wailing; now we may give ear to the utterances of the sages, and again only to the quarrels of drunken men; there are moments when we may take delight in all the pleasures that the world affords, but, anon, we may find that our bodies are covered with diseased sores: so is the life of man partly made up of nectar and partly of poison.

124. You disguise your voice and limbs like the actors in a play, and then flatter your wealthy patrons. But what part will you play at the time when your hair is grey with age?

125. Fortune, breath, wealth: all are transitory; righteousness is the only immovable thing in the world.

126. Hara, whose brow is ornamented by the crescent moon as by a tongue of flame, who absorbed like a moth the god of love that flew round him, thus showing himself at the zenith of his happiness, and who

removes the burden of darkness that takes possession of the earth; Hara, the gleaming light in the inner mind of the ascetic—may Hara overcome his enemies.

127. O mind of mine, pay no attention to the goddess of fortune, for she is as unstable as a courtesan, and as variable as the smile or the frown of kings. Nay, clothe thyself rather in ragged garments, proceed to Benares, and beg from door to door the food that men will gladly place in the receptacle you hold out to them.

128. The tortoise, whose back is bowed down with the weight of the great world which he carries upon it, has indeed justified his existence, and no less glorious was the birth of the polar star, for the splendid zone of the universe is fixed upon it. All other things that come into existence are as if dead; they fly about aimlessly, and their wings are useless in doing good to others: they are neither above like the star, nor underneath like the tortoise—they are even as petty insects, buzzing about the fig-tree of the world.

129. "My house is magnificent," says the man whose mind is darkened by igno-

rance; "my children are respected, my wealth is boundless, my wife is beautiful, and I am in the prime of life." The wise man, on the other hand, knows that everything in the prison-house of this world is but ephemeral, and frees himself from all its earthly possessions.

130. Those who wish to swear may do so; but we are righteous, and, as there is no evil in us, we cannot utter abusive words. We cannot expect of a man more than is in him, nor can we bestow upon him that which does not exist. We cannot give a hare's horn to anyone.[1]

131. Sustenance can be obtained in this world by easy enough means. The land is full of fruit. The skin of the elephant or the deer would furnish us with clothing, and the consequences of happiness or of unhappiness are identical. Who, therefore, casting away the true idea of the deity, would worship a deity blinded by the love of money?

132. Our minds are not always set on the tasks they are carrying out, so that although we have killed elephants by our good swords,

[1] See note to Niti Sataka, aphorism No. 5.

although we have put our enemies to the torture, although we have gratified ourselves by amorous dalliance on the couch of our beloved mistress, and although we may live near within the thundering noise of the Falls of the Himalayas: yet we have had no pleasure. Like the crows, we have spent our lives in greedily picking up the crumbs of food thrown to us by others.

133. Cease, O my mind, from wandering hither and thither, and rest for a time! That which has been decreed by fate cannot be warded off: therefore think not of the past, and trouble thyself not about the future: take delight only in those pleasures which come to thee and are gone without being sought.

134. Let thy hand serve thee as a drinking-cup; eat in peace the food thou hast begged; repose thyself wheresoever thou canst, and look upon the whole world as grass. Only a few men before thee have got rid of their earthly forms, and acquired a knowledge of the continuous happiness felt by the ascetic: a bliss which it is not difficult to gain by favour of Siva.

135. O my mind, thou hast not released

Bali from Paṭala;[1] thou hast not got rid of death; thou hast not taken the dark spots away from the moon, and thou hast not removed sickness from among mankind. Thou hast not supported the universe, even for a moment, and so relieved the weariness of Shesha. O my mind, art thou not ashamed to be honoured unjustifiably in a manner appropriate only to great heroes?

136. My mind wishes to become united with Siva, for in this way all the disquietude resulting from discussions on the meaning of the different shastras is swept away, while the emotions, calmed by the noble sentiments of the poets, are brought under control, and we are freed from the doubts that beset us.

137. Why do wretched men tolerate the miseries they are forced to undergo by waiting outside the doors of the rich when the fruits of the earth lie ready to hand, and there is no scarcity of trees in every wood; when the sweet, cool water of the sacred

[1] A virtuous king who became so powerful as to arouse the anger of the gods. Vishnu begged from him as much ground as he could cover in three strides; and, on the request being granted, he stepped over both heaven and earth in two strides. In view of Bali's virtues, Vishnu left him the lower region (Patala).

rivers is easy to obtain, and when delicate plants form a soft couch on which the body may repose?

138. I beg my food; the cow of plenty gives me milk, and my ragged garments, mean as they are, keep out the cold, while I worship Siva without pause. What do I care for worldly possessions?

139. All the great ascetics have declared that the life spent as a beggar is not wretched, for the beggar fears no losses; he is not possessed of envy, pride, or haughtiness; he is free from the innumerable troubles that beset mankind, and he obtains his food from day to day without any great difficulty. The life of a mendicant is a means of purification, approved of by the gods. It lays up treasure for us that will last for ever, and adds to our devotion for Siva.

140. The beggar who rests his body upon the earth, who looks upon the sky as his canopy, and the moon as his lamp, and who takes delight in the unity which has been brought about between himself and divine peacefulness, his brow fanned from all quarters by the winds of heaven, is like unto a

prince, despite his having freed himself from all desire for worldly wealth.

141. The pleasures of the world are as ephemeral as the varying ripples of the mighty river. Our life passes in a moment, and our days here are few. The joys of youth vanish away, and even the love of one's friends faileth. Wherefore let the wise man who knows full well that this world is a vain thing, and whose mind clearly perceives the evil side of earthly attractions, make every effort in his power to reach a condition of indifference.

142. Thou dost not look upon the face of the rich; thou dost not speak flattering words; thou givest no heed to the utterances of pride; thou dost not wander hither and thither in the hope of profiting thereby: but thou eatest in due season the fresh blades of grass and sleepest peacefully when it is time to sleep. Tell me, O deer, what penance thou hast practised that thou canst lead such a life of contentment.

143. Young women flee from the man whose hairs are grey with age, and the man who is enfeebled by senility. They keep far away from him, and avoid him as they would

the well used by the Chandals with the pieces of bone suspended over it.[1]

144. How often, O senseless man, do thy plans come to naught! Filled as thou art with folly, how often hast thou not desired to drink deep draughts of water from the mirage of this world! Since thou art now as confident as ever, and since thy mind, though it has received many a shock, has not been subdued, surely thy heart must be made of imperishable marble.

145. What will not the eyes of a woman accomplish! They will softly and quietly make their way into a man's heart and inspire him with infatuation, with delirium, with threats, and with felicity. What, indeed, will not the eyes of a woman accomplish?

146. The powerful lion feeding on the flesh of bears and elephants enjoys the pleasures of love only once in a twelvemonth, but the dove, picking up only morsels of hard rock, loves every day. How, I pray, can this be explained?

147. The ascetic who desires union with

[1] The Chandals are pariahs and outcasts, lower even than the Sudras.

Hara leads a life of peaceful calm with his mind fixed only upon one object. He lives in some sacred forest with only the deer as his companions, supporting his life on the fruits of the earth, and on the vegetables growing on the banks of the stream; while the flat surface of a rock serves him for a couch. His mind is fixed upon Hara, and the forest and the dwelling are one and the same thing to him.

148. The goddess utters sweet sounding words that please us more than honey or ghee; the syllables that fall from her lips fill us with delight. Let us but obtain our barley grain by begging, and so long as we can do that, we shall have no desire to seek wealth in a state of slavery.

CHAPTER III

THE SRINGA SATAKA

1. Fall down and worship the illustrious wielder of the flowery bow,[1] who compelled even the gods themselves to be the servants of antelope-eyed ladies; the youth whose curious deeds cannot be described in words.

2. Smiles, gestures, modesty, and coquettish glances, the face half-turned away, teasing, jealousy, quarrels, chaff—these are indeed the weapons of women, out of which they make a chain to bind down men.

3. Eyes cast down, sidelong looks, pretty eyebrows, soft words, modest smiles, artificial movements and postures of the body, a slow, indolent movement in walking—these things serve women equally well as ornaments and as weapons.

4. If once our fancy has been caught by

[1] Cupid.

women we shall never cast a look round us without seeing the world filled, as it were, with the sparkling glances of lotus-eyed navodahs [1]—glances which strike us at first by the movements of the beautiful eyebrows, and then, perhaps, by the modesty or shyness of the fair one, or by her timidity and laughing gracefulness, or the unsteady feelings displayed in those eyes, those fickle eyes, whose magnificence resembles the dark-blue lotus in full bloom.

5. A face that shames the splendour of the moon, eyes that surpass the beauty of the lotus, a complexion outshining even the lustre of gold, thick hair, blacker than the black bee, breasts that make us forget the twin domes on the forehead of an elephant, rounded hips, and a sweet voice —these are the natural ornaments of young women.

6. What is not handsome about young and beautiful maidens who are just entering on the threshold of womanhood? Their gently smiling faces, frank and innocent looks, their harmonious voices when we speak to them, and, when they walk, the delicate

[1] Young and newly married women.

movements of their limbs, like the trembling of lotus stems—these things are, one and all, unsurpassed in their loveliness.

7. What can be more beautiful for the lover to look at than the face of his antelope-eyed mistress smiling at him with unchecked passion? What can be more lovely for him to breathe than the breath of her mouth? What more beautiful for him to hear than her voice? What more beautiful for him to eat than the delicate ambrosia of her lips? What can be more lovely for him to touch than her soft body, and what more beautiful for him to think about than the image and grace of his adored one?

8. Who is there that is not conquered by the artless, timid glances of lovely and youthful women, the melodious tinkling of whose loose anklets and waistbelts puts to shame even the sweet tones of the swans?[1]

9. The charms of a lovely woman, whose body has been anointed with saffron, whose necklace swings gently with the rise and fall of her golden breasts, and from whose feet we hear the sweet sounds of her tinkling anklets: by making use of these things

[1] A favourite comparison in Sanskrit poetry.

what handsome woman cannot reduce a man to a condition of the most abject slavery?

10. All the best poets were wrong when they called woman weak. How can such an expression be applied to those whose star-like eyes subdued the hearts of Indra himself, and the other mighty gods?

11. Makaradhvaja [1] is truly the obedient slave of the beautiful woman who possesses a pair of fine eyebrows: for he consoles himself in all their labyrinths, and is ready at any moment to take the field in her service.

12. Thy well-combed hair, thy splendid eyes, with their arches curved almost to thine ear, thy two rows of teeth, entirely pure and regular, thy breasts adorned with beautiful flowers or necklaces of pearls—thus thy body, oh beautiful woman, inspires us with the liveliest emotion.[2]

[1] Cupid; the Indian God of Love.

[2] In the original the lady is compared to "calm and peaceful Yogi"—this being a play on the Sanscrit words which, when applied to the ear, the teeth, and the pearls, have a complimentary meaning, though they bear a different interpretation—such as "self-denying," or "pious"—when applied to the divine writings or to emancipated souls.

13. Oh, thou most charming maiden, where hast thou acquired thy knowledge of archery?—a magnificent knowledge indeed; for thou canst pierce the hearts of others merely by touching the strings of the bow, without using a single shaft.

14. Nothwithstanding the light from the bright lamps, the fires, the sun, the moon, and the stars, the whole world appears to me to be wrapped in the deepest gloom, because my fawn-eyed darling is no longer with me.

15. It is but natural that the voluptuousness of thy rounded breasts, thy trembling eyes, thy ever-moving brows, and thy rosy lips, should arouse amorous emotions in a man; but why is it that that thin line of hair which we can just see peeping forth *ex ventre tuo* should cause us so much more emotional discomfort?—that little line of hair that looks like a special mark of favour bestowed by the God of Love himself.

16. The delicate form of that beautiful woman resembles the constellation of the stars. Look at her neck and breasts, her face that puts the moon to shame, and her slow, dignified mien.

17. If any emotion is aroused in thy soul at the sight of the firm breasts, the rounded hips, and adorable face of that young woman, and if your desire is all for the voluptuous sights on which you have cast your eye, then practise the virtues; for, without this practice, the fulfilment of your hopes can never come to pass.

18. There is one question upon which we must make up our minds, having set aside all longing for the time being: Shall we devote ourselves to the nitambas (mountain caves) or to the nitambas (sexual charms) of young and beautiful women?

19. In this worthless world learned men have two alternative ways of enjoying themselves: they may either drink the ambrosia of knowledge and truth, or they may give themselves up to the society of charming women and of courtesans, whose amorous desires are awakened by the mere touch of the hand.

20. That woman may indeed be said to be made up of precious jewels; for her face is like the moonstone, her dark hair like sapphires, and her hands like rubies, with their red palms.

21. What cannot clever women do when once they take possession of the hearts of men? They can drive them mad, intoxicate or stupefy them with sympathy and love, mock them, threaten them, please them, and likewise worry them in a thousand different ways.

22. Behold the delicate form of that charming woman who is walking in the cool moonlight with slow and cautious step, resting now and then in the shade of the forest trees, and, with her shapely hand, drawing her veil over her face to shield herself from the rays of the moon.

23. So long as we do not view women too closely, we wish merely to glance at their handsome figures. When once this wish is gratified, however, we want to have her whole body in a loving embrace. And when that boon has been vouchsafed us, we pray that our bodies may be united for all eternity.

24. Who can truly be said to have secured a portion of ethereal bliss in this wretched world? Those, doubtless, who wear fragrant garlands of jasmine round their necks, rub the sweet saffron over their bodies, and

press close to their hearts the adored form of their beloved.

25. Our beloved one approaches us with lascivious movements and then shyly yields to our embraces. But, her desire once gratified, she sets aside all reserve, becomes more audacious, and gladly gives herself up to all the delicious pleasures of love.

26. What pleasure can be compared to that of drinking the nectar off the lips of our beloved mistresses as they lie with dishevelled hair and rosy cheeks, their bodies palpitating with the delights of love?

27. *Qui nictantibus oculis amatoriâ e pugna fit copulationis liquor, hoc insimul ut veram lascivi dramatis catastrophen amantium paria sane dignoscunt.* (Literal translation by H. Fauche.)

28. Impotence is an unworthy thing that results in men, when they have become old, too old for the joys of love; but it never happens in the case of well-developed women: even when, in other respects, they have become old and enervated, they are still ready for pleasure.

29. The true object of amorous intercourse is the uniting of the hearts of the two

participants in it; and when this end is not accomplished the union resembles merely the contact of corpses.

30. How well women can charm men by their words—words which meekness may make sweet, or which may be affectionate, or slowly uttered as the result of the intensity of the woman's love, or agreeable to the ear, or expressive of the utmost happiness, or graceful, or passionate.

31. You must make your choice of a habitation—either on the banks of the Ganges, the holy waters of which will wash away all your sins, or on the breast of a beautiful young woman adorned with a necklace of pearls.

32. The anger of jealousy may rise in the hearts of the young women who love us, but it will last only until it is blown away by a fresh breeze bringing with it the sweet odours of the sandal-wood.

33. Who can avoid feeling the pleasurable excitement of passion in the course of a lovely spring evening when the air has an agreeable perfume, the boughs of the trees are covered with fresh foliage, and the sweet notes of the birds melt the hearts of the

ladies—and when, too, the wistful sigh and the gently moving breasts betray their amorous desires?

34. When lovers are separated from their sweethearts their feelings are made even sadder by the freshness of the spring, despite the songs of the birds and the magnificent breezes from the Malaya. In man's misfortunes even his nectar becomes poison for him.

35. Not many people can manage to delight themselves in the pleasant nights of Chaitra[1] by resting from the pleasures of love at the side of their adored ones or listening to the sweet notes of the cuckoos, by reposing within a lovely arbour of creepers, by entering into converse with good poets, or enjoying the cool rays of the moon.

36. The troubles of the traveller who is journeying far from home are added to by the sight of the burning mango stalks, representing, as it were, the burning flames of the fire of separation from his wife. Then, too, there are the sad notes of the birds and the sweet breezes blowing from the Malaya.

[1] From about the end of March to the middle of April.

37. In the springtime, when the scent of perfume pervades everything, and the atmosphere is heavy with the sweet odours of the mango flowers and the bees intoxicated with drinking the juice, we feel an irresistible desire to seek the society of those we love. Is there, indeed, any man who does not feel his heart moved by the impulses of love and passion?

38. Various things all help to strengthen, in the summer-time, the power of high spirits and love—the hand of a beautiful woman dripping with the moisture of sandal-wood, houses provided with artificial fountains of water, flowers, the rays of the moon, the mild and sweet-smelling breezes, and the beautiful roofs of the palaces.

39. When the privileged few are troubled by the excessive heat of summer they have remedies at hand—beautiful bunches of flowers, fans, the rays of the moon, pollen dust, charming lakes, sandal-powder, pure sidhou,[1] light clothing, fine palaces, and loving women with voluptuous eyes.

[1] Sidhou: Wilson defines this as "rum distilled from molasses."

40. A well-cleaned house, the spotless rays of the moon, the lotus-like faces of our adored ones, sweet-smelling sandal-wood dust, and beautiful flowers: all these things excite the hearts of the passionate, but they have no effect on the wise man who has turned his head away from the pleasures of love.

41. Who is not delighted by the rainy season—those months of autumn that rouse the passions of men, almost as much as a youthful woman, by the jati flowers which it brings to their full growth, and the clouds, thick with rain, like a full-breasted woman.

42. The feelings of everyone, whether happy or unhappy, are sure to be influenced and made somewhat melancholy by the sight of the cloudy autumn sky, the sprouting fields, and the fragrant breeze, heavy with the sweet odours of the kutaja[1] and the kadambs[2] and the peacocks that make the forest ring with their shrill cries.

43. When the traveller looks up and finds that the rain-clouds cover his head

[1] Nauclea orientalis.

[2] Echites antidysenterica (Fauche).

like a canopy, that the amorous peacocks dance on the sides of the mountains, and that the soil under his feet is beginning to be covered with budding flowers and roots, how can he refrain from uttering a sigh of melancholy pleasure?

44. Consider the case of beautiful and passionate women when they are separated from their husbands in the autumn: how lonely their days will be! and how will it be possible for them to walk abroad and see here the brilliant flashes of lightning in the sky, and there the peacocks, with their passionate cries, while sweet breezes blow about them and they feel the strong scent of the flowers?—when, in short, everything about them stimulates amorous passion?

45. In the dark nights of Nabhas or Shravana,[1] when the rain and the hail fall to the earth with a hideous noise, when the roads are flooded and the skies are continually illuminated with flashes of lightning: then women will be filled with miseries and fears and will long for the return of their loved ones.

46. For happy husbands a rainy day is a

[1] About July.

time of pleasure and delight, for, not being able to go out on account of the wet, they gladly return to their wives, who, trembling with cold, take them into their embraces.

47. He who is tired of the pleasures of love after part of the night has elapsed, and, his throat parched with unquenched thirst, sits on the lovely roof of a palace and yet refrains from the delight of drinking the clear autumnal water held to his lips in a pitcher by the hands of his beautiful sweetheart—she whose strength has also failed as the result of the pleasures of love—is without doubt a very unfortunate being.

48. Those persons are indeed fortunate who, in the depths of winter, can afford to have plenty of milk and ghee on their tables, wear thick garments, enjoy the luxury of anointing their bodies with saffron, tire themselves with a variety of sensual enjoyments, sleep in the embraces of beautiful women, and repose at their ease within their dwellings, chewing a leaf of piper-betel mixed with various spices.

49. Kissing the rosy cheeks of women, causing a feeling of cold on their faces over

which the luxuriant hair is blown hither and thither, moving even their breasts and blowing aside the clothing from their legs and bodies—clearly in doing all these things the winds of winter are playing the part of paramours with beautiful women in the broad light of day.

50. The winter wind tosses women's hair from side to side, makes them close their eyes, blows their garments hither and thither, thrills their bodies, embraces them, makes them utter low sounds of fear and delight, and kisses their lips; and in doing all this it acts with all the charm of a lover.

51. No doubt sensual pleasures lead to no good result, and prevent us from properly renouncing the world. People may think and speak thus, but there is nevertheless something powerful and, indeed, indefinable, in sensuality; something that can even agitate the souls of those who have turned away from the world to devote themselves to meditation and the search for truth.

52. You, for your part, have found consolation in studying the divine Vedic writings, while we, on the other hand, are

the disciples of poets whose words are always pleasing. You will therefore hold that there is nothing better on this earth than doing good to others, while we shall maintain that there is nothing better than lotus-eyed, beautiful women.

53. Of what use are vain words and useless discourses? There are only two things in this world to which man should give himself up. One is the youthful period of a beautiful woman, who is tired, so to speak, of carrying the weight of her lovely breasts and wishes for a new source of enjoyment, and the other is a forest where one can live as a hermit.

54. Listen, oh man, for I am saying what is true, and am not speaking frivolously. It is admitted and certain that nothing enchants the soul so much as young women. They alone are the cause of evil; and there is no other.

55. The lamp of wisdom and judgment in the hearts of man burns only so long as it is not extinguished by the brilliant glances from the eyes of beautiful women.[1]

56. Those learned men who interpret

[1] That is, women annihilate all discretion in man.

the Vedas by preaching that we should renounce the world do not, after all, preach this doctrine to us but with their tongue; for who can give up altogether the pleasure to be found in the society of a beautiful woman, ornamented with a waistbelt of precious stones?

57. That learned man who shuns the company of beautiful women is deceiving himself as well as deceiving others; for is it not the case that the enjoyment of apsaras[1] is one of the most prominent rewards of Heaven?

58. There are many men on this earth who can cleave in the brow of a mad elephant, and there are others who do not hesitate to go out and slay a lion; but who among the bravest can I point to as having broken the onslaught of the God of Love? Men of this last type are undoubtedly few.

59. A man may walk in the right path, retain control over himself, and behave with perfect propriety until at last he finds himself in the company of sparkling-eyed women who shoot arrows of love into his

[1] The Indian equivalent of Moslem houris.

heart from the bows formed of their beautiful eyebrows.

60. When women, inspired by the passions of love set about some task, even Brahma himself is afraid to place an obstacle in their way.

61. A man will preserve his greatness, wisdom, nobility, and learning until the God of Love causes his frame to tingle with the arrows of desire.

62. There are many profound students of the shastras, men who are famous for their morality and, indeed, for the knowledge they possess of their souls; but of the large number only a relatively small number can expect to reach eternal happiness; for the key of the arched brows of beautiful women opens a way for them leading to the gates of hell.

63. Identical with aphorism No. 18 of the Vairagya Sataka.

64. Foolish men have broken the divine seal of women. They have thrown it aside carelessly and now seek, but in vain, a substitute for this seal, which gives birth to love and brings everything to perfecting. But they have met with condign punish-

ment at the hands of Cupid himself. He has condemned some of them to walk to and fro in a naked condition and with their heads shaved, while others, with matted beards, beg their bread from door to door, carrying in their hand a human skull.

65. Even Visvamitra, Parashara, and innumerable other ascetics who had subsisted on little else than the winds of Heaven, dead leaves and water, were thrown into confusion at the mere sight of a woman as beautiful as the lotus; and how, then, is it possible for men living on luxuries such as rice, ghee, milk, and so forth, to control their senses? It would be as difficult for them to do so as it would be for Mount Vindhya to swim over the sea.

66. Had there been no young women with eyes as beautiful as the lotus and faces outshining the beauty of the moon, whose waistbelts gave forth such joyful sounds and who were almost bent by the development of their breasts, how would it have been possible for men to have cast aside their natural wisdom and inclinations and entered the service of some cowardly king,

passing their time near the gates of the palace?[1]

67. If there had been no beautiful women in the world, no wise man would have stained his head by devotional bows, particularly when he could have spent his time in some saintly cavern on the side of the Himalayas, whose rocks are washed by the waters of the Ganges and whose trees have their roots in the shoulders of the Nandi, the divine Ox of Siva.

68. It would have been an easy matter to pay for our passage over the ocean of existence if there had been no women with beautiful eyes to hinder our progress.

69. No one in this world, O king, has ever succeeded in crossing his ocean of desires. Of what use to us are abundant riches if we must let our youth slip away from us without the enjoyment of our wives whom we adore? Let us therefore hasten to our homes so that we may be able to reach them before the beauty of our loved ones has been withered by the approach of age.

[1] That is, most men enter such service as this simply for the sake of their wives and children.

70. What greater calamity can a man suffer in this world than his own youth, which is at once the abiding-place of passion, the cause of dreadful agonies in hell, the seed of ignorance, the gatherings of clouds that hide the moon of knowledge, the great friend of the God of Love, and the chain that binds together innumerable sins.

71. Fortunate indeed is the person who can retain the mastery of his senses at the critical period of his youth—youth, this waterer of the tree of love, the rapid-flowing stream of sexual enjoyment, the dear friend of the God of Love, the full moon of the chakor-like eyes of women, and the treasury of happiness and wealth.

72. "Beautiful woman. What a divine expression! What a magnificent form!" cries the man who is blinded by passion; or, perhaps, "What a breast! What eyebrows!" In this way the sight of a beautiful woman delights him. He feels intoxicated with an excessive joy, and yet he may know very well that she is a woman whose impurity is known to the whole world.

73. How can we go on loving women

when the thought of her warms our hearts, the sight of her intoxicates us, and a touch of her nearly drives us mad?

74. A woman is indeed the very incarnation of the purest ambrosia so long as we have her within sight; but no sooner is she beyond the range of our vision than she becomes worse even than poison.[1]

75. Whatever young woman we may have in mind she is neither ambrosia nor poison—if she loves us she will be like an ambrosial creeper embracing us with its tendrils; but if she is indifferent she is like a poisonous plant.

76. A whirlpool of uncertainty, a palace of pride, a prison of punishment, a storehouse of sin, a fraud in a hundred different respects, an obstacle placed for us before the gates of paradise, the field of deceit, a basket of illusion, the open throat of hell: such are some of the features of women, who change nectar into poison and are as a chain by which man is attached to the chariot of folly.

77. It is certain enough that the face of a

[1] The company of our wives is delightful, and separation from them is as bad as poison.

woman is not made up of the moon, that her eyes are not twin lotuses, and that her limbs are not really gold. Why, alas, have poets been led to deceive us in this manner? Men are capable of distinguishing; but nevertheless, deceived by the poets, they none the less adore those fawn-eyed women, even though they know well enough that their bodies are composed of nothing more than skin, flesh, and bone.

78. Redness is a natural feature of the lotus; but the bees mistake it for a sign of its love for them, so they continually hover around the flower. Similarly, though flirtations and amorous actions are natural to women, they yet make deep impressions on the hearts of foolish men, who mistake these things for real tokens of love.

79. We behold a young girl with a lotus-eyed face resembling the splendour of the moon, and we remark the ambrosia on her lips. Too soon this face, like a rotten piece of fruit, will lose all its flavour, and will begin to taste like bitter poison.

80. A young woman is like a river; for the lines of her body resemble the waves; her breasts represent the ducks swimming

on the surface, the nymphs are seen in the brilliant colours of her face: but the bed of the river is dangerous, its course is difficult to perceive and leads rapidly to the ocean; so let men turn aside from it if they do not wish to be drowned.

81. Women, being all of a flighty disposition, look at this man and talk to that man at one time—and think of yet a third person: Who can possibly be a lover of women?

82. Women's words may be like honey, while their hearts may be filled with poison. What more natural, then, than we should clasp their breasts tightly while kissing their lips?

83. Oh my friend! Carefully avoid that form of serpent whom we know as woman. She wears the hood of amorous glances and actions while the looks she darts from her eyes are like stings of poison. Those who are bitten by ordinary snakes may be cured by medicines; but those who are wounded by the serpents in the form of woman cannot be cured even by the most famous charmers.

84. Cupid, in the guise of a fisherman,

has spread his net in the form of a woman; and the bait he offers is the nectar from her lips. Soon men are tempted by the attraction that is put before them and, when they are caught, they are roasted in the fire of love.

85. Never, oh my heart, venture into the dense forest of a pretty woman's body. The way through it is rendered difficult by the high mountains of her breasts, and the God of Love hovers round like a brigand.

86. Woe is me! for I must one day be pierced by the large, swift, voluptuous eye of a woman, which follows one like a quickly-moving serpent, and finally strikes. In nearly every country there are charmers who can cure a snake bite; but, alas! for the man whose heart is pierced by the eye of a woman there is neither medicine nor doctor.

87. In one place we hear a melodious song, in another we see a well-executed dance or inhale a beautiful perfume; while again, somewhere else, we are intoxicated by touching a beautiful breast. In this way our senses ramble hither and thither and destroy the higher ideas of our minds—all of them

workmen carrying out useless tasks and all of them continually abused and deceived.

88. The disease of love cannot be healed by mantras or the customary medicines. The study of the divine texts is of little avail; and whenever the patient is attacked his eyes roll with pain, and his limbs assume a peculiar livid hue.

89. What wise man can possibly take delight in loving a prostitute—a woman who, for the mere hope of gaining a small sum of money, sells her lovely person even to a blind man, or a man who is indescribably ugly and worn out with age, or a man of low origin, or again a man who repels us by his leprosy. What man, I ask, can love a prostitute—this scythe who cuts down the divine shrub of wisdom, the roots of which are planted in paradise itself?

90. A prostitute is, so to speak, a fire of love, glowing from the fuel of beauty, and burning to ashes the youth and wealth of sensual persons.

91. However beautiful the lips of a prostitute may be, no man who respects himself can possibly kiss them—for what are they but a kind of vessel in which everyone is at

liberty to spit, be he spy, soldier, thief, slave, actor, or cheat?

92. Happy indeed are those men whose hearts are not inflamed by the sight of beautiful women with large eyes, firm breasts, and all the characteristics of youth about their delicate bodies.

93. My child, why dart coquettish glances from thy half-closed eyes? Cease! Cease! for thy labour is in vain. We have become different men; our youth is at an end. The world, so far as we are concerned, is in the middle of a forest. Folly is dead in our hearts, and this world, through which one's desires are inflamed, is to us nothing but a handful of grass.

94. That charming young woman continually casts sparkling glances towards us; but what object can she have in doing so? Our desires have long since left us, and love, the tireless hunter, has put away his arrows which pierce our bodies with the pangs of pain. Yet that woman will not cease. [*Cf.* Vairagya Sataka, aphorisms Nos. 66 and 67.]

95. Magnificent palaces, passionate young women, wealth, and power—a man can enjoy

these things in recompense for virtuous actions, but only for so long as the merits of such actions entitle him to do; and then, when the term has expired, everything collapses and vanishes into ruin like a rope of pearls suddenly broken in the course of an amorous dispute.

96. Love, who, although invisible, attacks everybody, continually hovers round the victorious ascetic in whose soul all evils have been conquered by meditation and the practice of Yoga. In view of this, what use can he make of the society of agreeable women, the charming honey of their lips, the odour of their sighs, and their voluptuous kisses?

97. Why, O love, should you tire yourself? of what avail now your bow and arrow, or your words uttered in your most melodious tones? Away from me, young fool, away with your side-glances so piercing, sweet, loving, and delicate! My thoughts are directed now only towards God; the only ambrosia which I absorb is that which comes to me when I meditate at the feet of Siva!

98. When I was ignorant and walking in darkness it appeared to me that the whole

world was nothing but the body of a woman; but now that I have become more clear-sighted, I recognise that the three worlds are comprised in Brahma himself.[1]

99. One man walks in the path of absolute renunciation, while another follows the way of moral obligations, and a third devotes himself to love.

100. It is thus in this world that the differences in the characters of men enable us to distinguish between them; and if the third does not possess what, in love, is essentially beautiful, the wishes of the second tend towards the beautiful. The soul of the first has not yet reached this stainless state; nevertheless his desires have gained possession of the lotus.

[1] *Cf.* Niti Sataka, aphorism No. 8.

A NEW LIBRARY OF EASTERN THOUGHT AND LETTERS.

LITERATURE AND PHILOSOPHY OF THE ORIENT.

THE PUBLISHER begs to announce the issue of a new series of translations from the masterpieces of Oriental Philosophy and Literature. His aim is to issue, at a reasonable price, complete, and not merely abridged, translations of such well-known works as the Dhammapada, the Hitopadesa, the Upanishads, etc., etc., which have hitherto been accessible to the English reader only in incomplete or else somewhat expensive forms. Except in the case of a few of the longer works, each volume of the series will be complete in itself, and will be provided with an Introduction, and, where necessary, notes by Mr J. M. Kennedy, author of "Religions and Philosophies of the East," "The Quintessence of Nietzsche," etc.

THE "SATAKAS" OF BHARTRIHARI forms the first volume of the series, and other volumes in contemplation are:—

(2) "THE KATHAKOSHA OR TREASURY OF FABLES, TALES AND STORIES."

(3) "THE BUTTRIS - SHINGHASHUN, OR THIRTY-TWO IMAGES," a series of Hindu Tales.

(4) "THE PANCHA TANTRA." (The tales which form the basis of the well-known fables of Pilpay and of many of the stories found in "The Arabian Nights.")

(5) "THE HITOPADESA." A wonderful collection of Hindu moral tales, containing many shrewd observations on life and conduct.

The early volumes of the series will consist mainly of translations from Indian literary and philosophical works; but later on translations from the Persian, Arabic, Hebrew, Chinese, and Japanese will be added, thus making the series representative of every department of Eastern thought and letters.